Ada C. Chaplin

Our Gold-mine

The Story of American Baptist Missions in India

Ada C. Chaplin

Our Gold-mine
The Story of American Baptist Missions in India

ISBN/EAN: 9783744791144

Printed in Europe, USA, Canada, Australia, Japan

Cover: Foto ©ninafisch / pixelio.de

More available books at **www.hansebooks.com**

OUR GOLD-MINE.

THE STORY OF

AMERICAN BAPTIST MISSIONS IN INDIA.

BY

MRS. ADA C. CHAPLIN,

AUTHOR OF "CHRIST'S CADETS," "CHARITY HURLBURT," ETC.

"There is a gold-mine in India; but it seems almost as deep as the centre of the earth. Who will venture to explore it?" — ANDREW FULLER.

"I will go down; but remember that you must hold the ropes."— WILLIAM CAREY.

MISSION ROOMS, BOSTON:
W. G. CORTHELL, PUBLISHER.
1877.

Stereotyped and Printed by
Rand, Avery, and Company,
117 Franklin Street,
Boston.

PREFACE.

To the Members of my own Bible-Class and of other Bible-Classes: —

I HAVE written this book for you; not for those who have lived through, and helped make, the history it records, for they do not need it; not for those who feel *no* interest in the work it describes, for they will not read it; but for you, all of whom, I think, feel some interest in the great conflict waging between the kingdoms of good and evil for the possession of our world.

If it shall make more real to any one of you that part of the battle-ground which lies beyond our immeate vision, if it shall awaken in any heart a thought of earnest sympathy for our brethren of other races, if it shall make any faltering step steady and true for the Master, I shall not regret having written it.

Should this little work be read by any already at all

familiar with its subject, I know it will be with a sense of disappointment at the slight notice given to many names familiar and dear to them, and to departments of the work in which they are especially interested. In view of the small compass of the book, the necessity for explaining many things to those unfamiliar with its subject, and its aim to be a record of the work rather than a biography of workers, this disappointment was inevitable. It is fully shared by the author.

If, in becoming more intimately acquainted with them than in any other way would have been possible, I was at first startled by the discovery that missionaries, heathen, and ourselves were made of the same original material, I can nevertheless say, that day by day, as I have studied the lives of those who are doing our work in foreign lands, my reverence for them has increased, and for none more than for those whose names are hardly mentioned in these pages, but whose work, though more hidden from our sight than that of others, fills not less space in the record-book of heaven.

A. C. C.

CONTENTS.

CHAPTER		PAGE
I.	THE DARKNESS BEFORE THE DAWN	7
II.	BRAHMANISM AND ITS ADVERSARIES	30
III.	THE FIRST MISSIONARIES	43
IV.	JUDSON AND BURMAH	63
V.	THE FIRST BURMAN CHRISTIANS	81
VI.	IN PRISON	106
VII.	THE WILD MEN	122
VIII.	JUNGLE AND CITY	138
IX.	SHADOW AND SUNLIGHT	177
X.	NEW FIELDS.—TOUNGOO, SHWAYGYEEN, HENTHADA	195
XI.	RENEWED FIELDS.—RANGOON, BASSEIN, PROME,	226
XII.	TAVOY, MAULMAIN, AND THE SHANS	259
XIII.	ASSAM.—BRAHMANISM AGAIN	293
XIV.	THE TELUGUS	337
XV.	TO-DAY	372

OUR GOLD-MINE.

CHAPTER I.

THE DARKNESS BEFORE THE DAWN.

"I WISH I was in China!"

"So do I!"

The door closed with a slam after the last speaker, a boy of fourteen, and then opened again of its own accord, as doors are wont to do when school-boys close them.

"Then you'd be a mithunary, Katie," lisped a little four-year-old, who sat on the floor, drawing all sorts of ungeometrical figures with a bit of charcoal carelessly dropped there.

"I think I could be thankful that I'm not one of the 'poor heathen,' in that case," responded Walter Bancroft, closing the door again, and this time firmly.

Katie's cheeks flushed. She wiped the last plate vigorously, and put it with its fellows on the table. Then she let the wiping-cloth hang loosely on her arm, and turned toward the window, looking not through it, but out of another window, that opened into her own future; and there she saw only a long vista of unwashed plates, pots and kettles, unswept floors, and ragged garments, all looking to her to be put in order. She had taken this same view often; but that did not make it more pleasant. Life looked very long to Katie at fifteen.

"This is too bad, Katie, standing by the window with your dish-pan not washed, your dishes not set away, and little Minnie covering herself with charcoal." The words were spoken in a low, gentle voice, by a very sweet-looking young lady; but they brought to Katie Marshfield's cheeks the same hot flush that had died away with Walter's last retreating footstep.

Katie bit her lips, washed the pan, set away the dishes rapidly, then leaned her head upon the table, and burst into tears.

Katie Marshfield was a minister's daughter. She understood a little music, a little drawing, a little mathematics, a good deal of embroidery and crochet-work (of all of which she was fond), and a little housework (of which she was decidedly not fond). Shall we say, too, that she understood a little of religion, or rather, that, with a heart warm with love for Christ, she failed to see that this, as well as all our other mind and soul treasures, was designed not merely for enjoyment, but for use? She had many dreams of doing and suffering great things for Christ; but it had never come into her mind to do and suffer little things for his sake. And so, while her religion sustained her most beautifully in the dark hour of her father's death, it seemed not to help her greatly in washing dishes, and sweeping floors, and taking care of little Minnie, which was her main work in the family, where, for the three weeks since the funeral, her lot had been cast.

Ida Southworth, Mrs. Bancroft's sister, was so very quiet, so very practical, so abundant in every virtue that Katie lacked, that she liked her even less than she did the impulsive Walter, who was very much what Katie herself would have been, if she had been a boy, and had not been a Christian, and who, for three weeks, had been the chief torment of her life. Mrs. Bancroft everybody loved. Walter's cousin Charles, who professed to live in the next house, but really took his meals there, and lived wherever Walter was, was one of the boys who, taking color readily from their surroundings, are rarely found fault with. Little Minnie, and Edith, three years older, were Katie's idols; and these few people were all of the great world with which she had much to do, except in day-dreams.

"Oh, I wish I *was* a missionary!" she exclaimed; and her tears flowed afresh. It was not the first time she had said this. The longing came to her often, and always filled her with contempt for the seemingly insignificant duties that lay around her. She had no idea that the larger part of the missionary's work lay also in little things. To her imagination it was something wholly great and glorious. Now, as her mind rested upon it, her tears dried away; so that, when Mrs. Bancroft entered the room, she was only thinking.

"What are you thinking of, Katie?" The words were in a tone of inquiry, not of reproof, though Minnie was still on the floor, unconsciously transferring to her dress the charcoal diagrams she had been drawing.

"Of being a missionary some time," Katie answered truthfully.

"If you would like to fit yourself for that work, I will give you all the help I can; but take care of Minnie now."

Katie took off the soiled garments, washed the little black hands, thinking meanwhile of other hands, many miles away, from which the black could never wash off, and of souls darker than the bodies that cover them, that might be cleansed by the blood of Christ. "That would be *real* work, something worth living for," she thought, as she led the now presentable little Minnie into the sitting-room.

"How would you like to take the missionaries as the subject for our evenings this winter, Katie?" asked Mrs. Bancroft.

"I should like it above all things," Katie exclaimed enthusiastically.

"It seems to me that something a little more practical would be better just now," said Ida as Katie left the room. "That child has no idea of the duties of her present situation; and I think there is real danger in talking with her about these things, that will only encourage her dreamy, unsettled disposition, and unfit her for any real work in life."

"Perhaps so," answered Mrs. Bancroft, two words which are usually effective in shutting off further discussion; and so the subject was dropped till all were gathered around the evening lamp.

"Well, mother, what next? We've done up the Romans and the Reformation," said Walter, alluding to previous evening talks.

"We are going to talk about the heathen and the missionaries," said Katie a little triumphantly.

"The heathen are well enough; but I detest the missionaries," answered Walter, as usual saying something a good deal worse than he meant.

"I don't." Kate would probably have answered any other remark of Walter's with "I don't," she was so much in the habit of it; but she was in earnest this time.

"You wouldn't say that, if you knew, Walter," interposed Charlie. "Why, it's just like a fairy-tale, some of it."

"Well, I hate fairy-tales."

"But how they get into tigers' dens, you know, and how the alligators catch them,— I say it's interesting."

"But the alligators don't catch most of them, unfortunately; and those that are left are real stupid."

"How much do you know about them?" asked Mrs. Bancroft quietly.

"Nothing, except that they have dark complexions, and wear spectacles. I saw one of them on a platform once, but did not stay to hear him speak."

Walter joined in the laugh that followed this frank confession; and Mrs. Bancroft began her story, promising, however, that she would only tell about the heathen this time, and the missionaries should wait till they were called for.

"More than three thousand years ago, while Samson was catching foxes and telling riddles in Palestine, or perhaps still farther back, while Moses was writing his wonderful songs and telling the story of the world's creation, there were hymn-writers in India. Nothing is left of them now but their names, their language, and their hymns; but from these we can learn a great deal about the people themselves, and something about their ancestors and ours a great deal farther back."

"And ours, mother?" exclaimed Walter.

"Yes; for their ancestors were ours too; and these people, whose story you shall hear, are our distant cousins.

"In that very early time, when bears and deer and squirrels ran at large in the forests that grew where London and New York are now, our Eastern cousins had ploughs and carts, and oxen to draw them, and roads and inns for travellers. They used gold money, and gambled for it, and spent it in getting drunk, very much like some of their distant relatives in the nineteenth century. They had temperance writers too, and men who abhorred gambling. Trade, dress, jewels, and fast horses, had each their devotees among these far-away cousins, as among us. They had figures too; and no doubt their merchants kept accounts."

"Did they have slates and slate-pencils, and go to school?" asked Edith.

"That is more than I can tell you. More likely they ciphered on palm-leaves."

"But how do you know what you have told? I shouldn't think their hymns would be about such things," asked the incredulous Walter.

"Suppose, three thousand years from now, every book in our language were blotted out, except our hymn-books. Suppose that then some refined and educated Fijian or Esquimau should read such hymns as this : —

> 'Had I the tongues of Greeks and Jews,
> And nobler speech than angels use,
> If love be wanting, I am found,
> Like tinkling brass, an empty sound.'

Or this : —

> 'The children are gathering from near and from far:
> The trumpet is sounding the call to the war.'

From these two stanzas of two hymns, our Esquimau investigator could learn that the Americans of the nineteenth century studied foreign languages, knew something of ancient history, of the use of metals, of war, and of musical instruments. Even the 'golden hereafter' might be good for something then, in showing him that we lived in frame-houses built with 'rafters.' Now, if these few lines could tell him so much, you will easily see, that, with the whole hymn-book, he could learn how we live, what we are, and what we do, pretty thoroughly. In the same way, we learn what the East-Indians of Samson's time did and thought and were."

"But where were *we* then,— the English, I mean?" asked Charlie.

"I cannot tell; living in caves, and roasting each other for dinner in earth furnaces, perhaps, if the stories of some of our modern geologists are true."

"But what has made the difference?" asked Walter.

"I cannot answer that question without telling you something about the missionaries; and I promised not to do that to-night. I certainly cannot say, that if Christ had not sent out twelve missionaries with the command, 'Teach all nations,' I should to-night have been eating you, instead of talking to you. Probably I should not: for when Cæsar invaded England, more than fifty years before Christ was born, its people reserved all that kind of diet for their daintier gods; and even they were treated to a delicate young man or woman only on special occasions, and were expected to give full harvests, rain, or great victories, in return. Except on the coast, the people wore little clothing, and threw off that little when they went to battle, showing to their Roman invaders their naked bodies, tattooed and painted in what was the very height of London fashion two thousand years ago. The citizens of the country that now rules the wave paddled about in skin-boats; and, when our Eastern cousins had finished the hymns of the Vedas, the ancestors of Shakspeare and Milton had not even a written language. But it was not of English heathen that I meant to tell you. Most of the hymns of these early Hindoos, like most of ours, were prayers; and here, I think, is what is best of all, that, in reading them, we cannot help feeling that some of their authors worshipped the same God that we do, though calling him, as we do, by various names. Let me give you a specimen of some of these best hymns:—

'1. Let me not yet, O Varuna! enter into the house of clay: have mercy, Almighty; have mercy.

'2. If I go along trembling, like a cloud driven by the wind, have mercy, Almighty; have mercy.

'3. Through want of strength, thou strong and bright God, have I gone wrong: have mercy, Almighty; have mercy.

'4. Whenever we men, O Varuna! commit an offence before the heavenly host, whenever we break the law through thoughtlessness, punish us not, O God! for that offence.'

"In another, Varuna is described as —

'He who knows the place of the birds that fly through the sky, who on the waters knows the ships;

'He who knows the track of the wind, of the wide, the bright, the mighty, and knows those who reside on high;

'The God whom the scoffers do not provoke, nor the tormentors of men, nor the plotters of mischief.'

"Again they say that he 'perceives all wondrous things, and sees what has been and what will be done;' and one of these poets speaks distinctly of the oneness of God. 'They call him Indra, Mitra, Varuna, Agni: that which is One, the wise call him in divers manners.'

"You must not think that most even of the Rishis, these poets of whom I have been telling you, were worshippers of the true God. Among their hymns there are prayers to the sun, the dawn, the sky, the fire, and many others of the things that lead our thoughts away beyond themselves to God. How many of them stopped with the outward objects, how many looked through them to Him who made them, how far their immediate ancestors held a still purer faith, no one can tell. As I said, I have given you some of the best. Many of the hymns of the Veda are weak and childish.

"A few centuries passed by. The old form of

Sanscrit, in which the Vedas were written, had become as puzzling to the people of India as the old English I showed you last week was to you. Few could read, and fewer understand, the writings of the Rishis. Then those who understood them, or thought they did, wrote commentaries upon them: these are the Brahmanas. In a few centuries more, the Brahmanas had shared the fate of the poems, and other commentaries were written upon them: these are the Sutras. These old hymns, with the commentaries upon them, and the commentaries upon those commentaries, are called the Rig Veda; but properly the name belongs only to the hymns. Besides it, and in great part made from it, are three other Vedas of far more modern date."

"And are these what they call the Shaster?" asked Walter.

"In part. But, besides, there are the Ramayana and the Mahabarata, ancient epic poems; the Upanishads, theological treatises; the Laws of Manu, treating of almost every thing; the Puranas, a huge compendium of modern Hindooism, which probably had not reached its growth at the close of the sixteenth century"—

"That'll do, mother."

"But, before nearly all these had been written, there had been a great change among the countrymen of the Rishis. I suppose, like most great changes, it came so slowly, that nobody knew any thing was happening until the work was done. That change was the introduction of caste.

"If you were to go to India to-day, you would find soldiers who would throw away their dinner if but the shadow of one of their highest English officers fell upon it; because they, the soldiers, are of high caste, while the Englishmen are of no caste at all. You would find mothers having no quarrel with any of their neighbors, who yet, if a daughter should marry one of them, would drive her out of the house forever, because she had broken caste. You would find men who would rather starve than eat with our President or Queen Victoria; and all for caste."

"But how did this come about, mother?"

"As it may yet come about in America. Our Eastern cousins did not always live in India, but moved down there, probably from the North-west. I cannot tell when they came; but, before that, the land was filled with a race called the Dasyus, — dark-skinned, and not at all equal to our cousins the Aryans, who conquered them, killed many of them, and despised and hated those they let live. Often when I see an American boy pulling a young Chinaman's cue, or hallooing 'Paddy!' or pelting a little negro, I think, 'Just so, no doubt, the little Aryans teased the young Dasyus more than three thousand years ago, and never dreamed they were twining a rope around their country's neck that should lay it helpless for centuries.'"

"But, sister, you don't really think we are in danger of becoming Hindoos here in America?" asked Ida.

"Nothing can help it, so far as caste is concerned, but the missionary spirit of Christianity, teaching us to think souls as valuable in China, or Africa, or Ireland, as in America, now that our country is filling up with foreigners, many of them so unlike ourselves."

Walter gave a low, incredulous whistle; and Mrs. Bancroft continued: "There was another source of caste. There were priests, farmers, and soldiers among the people. The priests claimed the highest place, and took it. The soldiers came next; then the farmers. These formed three separate castes; but all joined in despising the poor Dasyus, now called Sudras. 'Do not speak to a Sudra,' says one of their authors; the gods do not: or, if you have something to say to him, speak to some other person standing by, and say, 'Tell this Sudra so.' So you see by this time the people had gods very unlike Him who 'dwelleth with him that is of a humble and contrite heart,' and who speaks in every human soul. Nobody but the Brahmans read the Vedas now, and they pretended that the Vedas, too, taught caste. Gods grew plenty, and silly stories were told about them. Hideous idols were made. Widows were forbidden to marry, and were taught to burn themselves with the dead bodies of their husbands. Time divided itself into four *yogas*, each counting its years by hundreds of thousands, together making up four million. The first was a golden one; but ever since, so the people were told, goodness had been dying out, until now, in the *Kali yoga*, nothing could be expected but a steady growth of wickedness. Above all, the people were taught to worship the Brahmans as a part of God himself. There was but one thing, so they thought, that common people needed to know; and that was to obey the Brahmans. If they did this, they might hope, after death, to be born into the world again human, and in some higher caste; failing, they must take the form of some lower animal. Some of these threatened transmigrations were ludicrously appropriate: for example, we read in the Laws of Manu, that, 'if a man steal grain, he shall be born a rat; if perfume, a muskrat; if flesh, a vulture; and so on indefinitely.'

"No wonder that atheistic teachers arose, and sceptics multiplied.

"Then came

"BUDDHA.

"His real name was Siddhartha, or perhaps Sakyamuni. He assumed the name of Gautama; and for his wisdom he was called 'The Buddha,' which means 'The Enlightened.' He was the son of a king, but left his native country and his kingdom, that he might seek for truth, or happiness, or something; for I doubt whether even he knew what he wanted. His soul was hungry, no doubt, as all souls are sometimes. He saw sickness, old age, and death around him; and his question was, 'How, since evil is everywhere, can we escape from evil?' The rabble of Brahman gods he despised and neglected: so some called him an atheist. He fasted, slept on rough beds, treated himself more severely than any Brahman: so his disciples called him a saint; but he himself claimed to be neither, for some time. If only then he had raised his soul to God, I doubt not that He, who perhaps at that very hour was speaking to Ezekiel or Daniel, would in some way have spoken to him; but he seems to have neither believed in God, nor disbelieved in him. Instead of looking to him for light, he looked to himself; and there he thought he found an answer to his question. It was this: All existence is evil, because changeable. If we believe rightly and do rightly, we shall at last enter *Nirvana*, and change no more.' In his five commandments he forbade lying, stealing, murder, drunkenness, and adultery. He rejected the Vedas and idol worship, and paid no attention to caste. What would he have said if he could have seen the time when three hundred and sixty-five millions of his followers should be bowing down to a hideous, long-eared, half-dressed image, and calling it Buddha, after himself, and when his own short creed and simple history should be stretched through more pages than are found in the Vedas and Puranas together!

"With this short creed he set out to convert India. Disciples flocked to him. He taught them to be kind to all human things: and he looked upon spiders and mosquitoes, and all living creatures, as human; for, like the Brahmans, he held that souls at death pass into other bodies; that the puppy of to-day may have been a gentleman yesterday, and may be a babe in our arms to-morrow. He taught them his five commandments, taught them to reverence himself, and, like him, to seek Nirvana. He grew old, and died. His disciples burned his body, fought for his bones, built eight temples to hold them, and called him God. If Buddha told the truth, he had entered Nirvana, and no longer knew, or felt, or cared for, any thing below. He did not wish praise or gifts; nor could he help his friends: but his disciples worshipped him, and made costly offerings to him, very much as if they did not believe a word he had said."

"But what is Nirvana?" asked Kate.

"Any thing you please, almost. To Buddha himself it meant, perhaps, not quite annihilation, but something so much like it, that our best scholars are puzzled to define the difference. In Buddha's own words, 'It is neither being, nor nothing.' It has the same meaning to many of the most intelligent Buddhists of to-day. Others speak of it as the incomprehensible, — the thing which is, but is not anywhere, which no one can understand. To others it means rest, freedom from thought, care, pain, and trouble. Meanwhile, many of the lower classes, looking through Nirvana's gates ajar, see there every thing they want to eat and drink, and to make them, in a coarse, gross way, happy."

"And did Buddhism grow after Buddha died?"

"Yes, very rapidly; and, in a few centuries, caste was little thought of. Brahmanism was scarcely visible; and all over India arose splendid temples to Buddha, the ruins of which still remain. There are curious carved images in them, and mounds of solid masonry; in one case, one hundred and six feet in diameter, and forty-two in height. In most of them are boxes of treasures and relics. Mr. Cunningham explored these topes some years ago, and opened the boxes. In many of them he found pearls, beads, wheat, barley, rice, and in one of them a live spider, probably a squatter on his own hook; though, if Buddha's doctrine be true, he was certainly the most valuable treasure in the box, since he alone contained a human soul.

"For nearly a thousand years, Buddha ruled India. Then the Brahmans again gained power. How they first gained it history does not tell us; but, when once it was theirs, they used it in driving the Buddhists into Ceylon, Nepal, Thibet, and China: and now in all Hindostan there are no Buddhists, and the ruins of these temples are the only witness left of one of the grandest failures of history.

"In the downfall of Buddhism, India learned, what our own country may yet have to be taught, that the soul can never find rest in a god who neither knows nor feels nor cares for us; that no talk about the 'divine possibilities of humanity,' even though coupled with a promise that every faithful soul shall at last become 'Buddha,' God, can atone for the loss of the right to say, 'Our Father who art in heaven.'

"I think it was the fact that the Brahman gods did feel, though not always very amiably, and did profess to take care, though certainly not very good care, of their followers, that gave them their second chance in Hindostan."

"I really think," said Ida, when she was left alone with Mrs. Bancroft, "that, in return for this gratification of Katie's missionary curiosity, you would do well on other evenings to compel her to spend a part of her time in some secular study. She is behind Walter now in mathematics, and doesn't know enough of geography or grammar to pass examination for the high school."

"I will think of it," said Mrs. Bancroft.

"And *insist* upon it, please; for, now her mind is turning so much to missionary studies, it will be harder than ever to persuade her to attend to these things, that have nothing to do with missions."

"I would like to see a study that had nothing to do with missions," replied Mrs. Bancroft. "I believe God made the world, knowing that it would be the field of missions; and that every object of nature, every science, physical and mental, and every art, was designed to pour its treasures into the missionary storehouse."

Ida smiled at what seemed to her a piece of enthusiastic extravagance not worth refuting.

CHAPTER II.

BRAHMANISM AND ITS ADVERSARIES.

"AUNTIE," said Charlie in one of his frequent vists to Mrs. Bancroft's sitting-room, "Clarence Merriam is coming to hear about the missionaries this evening."

"I don't want him; he's too big," spoke Edith.

"And a goose besides," added Walter.

"He knows a great many things you don't," Charlie answered warmly. Charlie was one who rather enjoyed being patronized by those who had stepped a few months beyond the limits of boyhood. Walter detested it. This was the occasion of their difference of opinion about Clarence.

"All geese know things that I don't," Walter retorted; "but I don't care to live in a poultry-yard for the sake of learning them."

"Clarence knows every thing already; that is his worst fault," said Katie.

"In that case he will not care to be with us often; and, since he has proposed to come, of course we must offer him a chair," said Mrs. Bancroft.

Early in the evening the chair was filled.

"Don't you think those Brahman gods must have had a jolly time, when they found themselves worshipped again, after being kicked around for half a dozen centuries or more?" said Walter, as the family were seated around the table, waiting for Mrs. Bancroft to come in from little Minnie's room.

"It isn't right for you to talk so. You know there are no *real* Brahman gods," said Kate.

"Besides, you ought to have more sympathy for poor Buddha," suggested Charlie.

"Oh! he had entered Nirvana, where he would rather enjoy being kicked round, or at least wouldn't have the slightest wish for any thing else. They have no desires of any sort in Nirvana, you know."

"And I should have told you," Mrs. Bancroft added as she sat down among them, "that, though Buddha has now no worshippers in his own country of Hindostan, a large part of the people of China, Nepal, Thibet, Siam, Burmah, and Japan, call themselves Buddhists now. To be worshipped by one-third of the people of the world would satisfy any ordinary ambition, one would think: but Buddhism in most of those countries is a very different thing from the doctrine that Buddha taught; and, if he were on earth to-day, I doubt if there is any place in the world where he would feel quite so much a stranger as in one of his own temples. No kitten ever tangled a ball of yarn more completely than Buddhism tangled the affairs of men and gods in India. Only two of the original castes could be found now, — the Brahmans and the Sudras; and a *pure* Sudra even was not very common. Most of the people were of mixed castes, each caste representing a different occupation. These distinctions had been little thought of while Buddhism ruled; but, when the Brahmans came back, they drew the lines more closely than ever, multiplying the number of castes to suit emergencies, until now it would puzzle a foreigner to count them."

"And did they bring back all the old gods too?" asked Kate.

"Yes, and more. If Hindoo gods were good for any thing, they would be the most profitable crop one could raise; for they multiply like thistles: no sooner is one planted than a dozen others shoot out from him. In this way, Juggernaut came from Krishna, and he from Vishnu, and all originally from Brahme, or the Brahma, of whom (or which), according to Hindoo theology, every thing we say is false: so it may be as well to say nothing.

"Among all their three hundred and thirty millions of gods, there was not one who loved them, not one whom they loved. Brahma, cold and unfeeling, ruled over all, but had no temples. Vishnu the preserver had a few; Siva the destroyer, many: but most worshipped the swarm of lower gods, who took care of harvests, health, weather, war, and other of the affairs of this life; and the worst gods had the most worshippers.

"And through all this great, wicked country rolled the beautiful, terrible Ganges, — the sacred Ganges, — rising far up among the Himalayas, amid scenery so full of God's glory, that one must be worse than a heathen who could visit it, and hear no voice calling upon him to pray;

dashing fiercely at first over its granite bed, then rolling on, through precipices and over crumbling rocks, unbridged through all its sixteen hundred miles, gathering, as it rolled, offerings of gold and silver and fruits, and animals, and children even, thrown into it by its worshippers, yes, and the lives of those worshippers, and their bodies when dead, mixing them with the filth of nine large cities, and uncounted villages, — yet still so sacred, that crowds of pilgrims flocked there to bathe, to drink its waters, to fill tneir dying mouths with its mud, or, it may be, to atone for the sins of a lifetime by dying beneath its waves. Near its source, in a region that seems more like the ruins of another world than a part of the home of mortals, are laid many of the scenes of the Shasters. In its lower course the Shasters find their true fulfilment. The River Ganges is the best commentary on Brahmanism."

"But how could there be such change from the original religion, when the people still had the Vedas, and believed in them?" asked Kate.

"The common people and the women were not allowed to read the Vedas. If a Sudra read them, he was to have his ears filled with melted lead. Few even of the Brahmans could read and understand them: and though remembering them removed all sin, and a Brahman who should destroy three worlds, and eat food from any quarter whatever, would be guiltless, if he remembered the Vedas, few remembered any parts but those used in sacrifice; and they ununderstood little of the meaning even of those.

"Here and there a Brahman might be found seeking absorption in Brahma; but since, in doing it, he must not only fight against every thing human within and around him, but against a whole swarm of lower gods, jealous lest he should just miss of absorption, enter heaven, and become a rival of theirs, his chance was not great. Too often he became contented with the reward he was sure he could obtain, — the praise, worship, and gifts of the people, — and, reserving his austerities for exhibition before the public, lived in private a life of luxury and vice. It was an essential article of his creed that every thing was unreal, and life an infinite humbug: what wonder that he often became a humbug too?

"The lower classes were hopeless. At the best, they could only gain absorption by being born Brahmans in some future transmigration. If they tried for any thing in the next life, it was only to have a tolerably comfortable body to enter when they should leave this. With a hundred thousand hells yawning to receive them, the chance of that was not great. But there was more hope of gaining it by making gifts to the idols or the Brahmans, or by digging pools, or making roads, or a thousand other things, than by truth and honesty."

Clarence Merriam showed some uneasiness during this description, and, when Mrs. Bancroft paused, interposed at once: —

"All you say may be true; but are there not some compensations in the heathen religions which we ought not to overlook? Do you not think our cold Western religion suffers from the lack of that feminine element which all other forms of worship share? Nowhere is the refining. influence of woman more needed than in religion; and I think the heathen in their goddesses, and the Catholic in his worship of the Virgin, have something that our balder Protestant faith sadly lacks."

Charlie gazed at Clarence in profound reverence while he delivered this brisk little speech.

Walter drummed on the table. Mrs. Bancroft listened as attentively and respectfully as if she had not heard the same thing a great many times before.

"As for the 'refining influence of woman,'" she answered, "there is a good deal of nonsense about it. Every thing depends upon who the woman is. Very possibly, however, we may learn something by paying a visit to Kali, wife of Siva, and most popular of Hindoo goddesses, in her home as it was when the deep quiet of Brahmanism was first broken by the advent of missionaries.

"Three miles out from Calcutta, we enter a low, filthy, ruinous archway. This leads us to a miserable court-yard; this, to another archway. On our way we pass numbers of fakirs, saying their prayers under the oshatto-tree, and looking wistfully to us for money as we go by. Then we reach a building smaller than the smallest English chapel, though larger than most Hindoo temples, the famous Kali Ghat. This is Kali's house. There she stands, a huge, black stone, with four hands, a hideous face, red eyes and nose, and a tongue projecting a foot from her mouth. Here she eats, sleeps, and receives the offerings of kids, buffaloes, rice, sweetmeats, fruits, gold, and silver, which her admirers bring her. Here, in 1802, the officers of the English Government brought her a thank-offering of five thousand rupees for their successes in India. Near by is a large hall, where attending Brahmans read the Shasters, and her friends meet to worship her. Now and then a stray cow or bull takes its place among them; but no one takes offence at it. Why should he? The cow is scarcely less sacred than the Brahmans, and much more so than those who listen to them. Twice a day she eats a meal of rice, sweetmeats, and fruit, so abundant, that she has to employ from thirty to a hundred people to chew and digest it for her. Every day she takes a nap. I am not aware that she does any thing besides eat and sleep now: but her pictures and images all over the land bear witness to the deeds she has done in times past; for her waist is girdled with the severed, bleeding hands of those she has slain; and on her breast rests a necklace of forty skulls. I cannot ask you to go to one of her feasts with me; for she is worshipped with songs so vile, that it would be a crime to listen to them: yet men, women, and children join the worship. Her admirers are everywhere. Thieves pray to her for success in thieving; honest men, for protection against thieves; merchants, for prosperity in business; mothers, for their children; lost women, for the sharers of their sin; and all bring her offerings. Many a rich man has made himself poor for her sake: and if, by chance, a poor man in the country villages offends the Brahmans, when he wakes in the morning he may find an image of Kali placed before his door; and then woe to him if he fail to beg, borrow, or steal money enough to 'worship her' by offerings of rice and sweetmeats and clothes, and brass vessels, to his tormentors! The Puranas say that the sacrifice of a goat pleases her a hundred years; of a man, a thousand; of three men, a hundred thousand: and careful directions are given for human sacrifices, with the promise, that, if the severed head of a victim smiles, prosperity will follow; and, if it speaks, whatever it says will come to pass. When Carey came, she had had no public human sacrifices for years; yet now and then, in the morning, before her temple, might be found cold, headless bodies. Whence they came no one told; but why they were there every one knew; and no one dared hint at the arrest of the murderer, lest Kali be angry. Long after Carey's time, Kali's pet children, the Thugs, men wholly consecrated to her service, roamed through India, clustering especially about holy Benares, lying in wait at night, and slipping the fatal noose over rich merchants, or pilgrims, or strangers who had been heard to speak a word against Kali, or any one who passed; passing their trade on from father to son, gaining in it such horrible skill, that no sound ever escaped the strangling victim, nor was his death known, till, in the morning, his body was found with tongue thrust from his mouth in hideous imitation of the goddess to whom he was sacrificed.

"They claim, that, in earlier times, Kali used to follow their bands, and herself eat up their victims: but one of their number, looking back, saw her at her repast, which so disgusted her, that she would act as sextoness no longer; but she gave them the hem of her garment for a noose, and a tooth for a pickaxe; and with terrible faithfulness has her hint been carried out.

"But is Kali pleased, after all? That question rests always like a nightmare upon her worshippers. Once a year most of the wealthier families make an image of her from straw and wood, and sacred Ganges clay; and a feast is spread; and Brahmans dance, and perform ceremonies, and pray the goddess to enter the image. At the close of the day they thank her for her visit, and allow her to leave again.

"They might well be thankful, if, for even one day, her spirit could be confined to clay images. It is everywhere. It broods, a terrible presence, over all India, always demanding gifts, always threatening vengeance, always hungry for blood. If a friend is sick or dying, if business fails, if floods come, Kali is angry; her temple is deluged with the blood of animals, or her altars covered with treasure; and, if she is still unsatisfied, the mother tears her infant from her, and — tearless, for the goddess hates sentiment — drowns it to appease her."

Mrs. Bancroft paused. There was a moment's silence, in which everybody was expecting everybody else to speak. Then Walter broke it:—

"Mother, haven't we had 'refining influence' enough for the present. Suppose we try missionaries next time?"

"They are ready, if called for," said Mrs. Bancroft.

CHAPTER III.

THE FIRST MISSIONARIES.

O more heathen for the present, Kate!" exclaimed Walter the next morning.

"Why not?"

"Grandpa Sears is coming."

"Who is grandpa Sears?"

"Mother's grandfather,— the one that brought her up when her father died."

"He must be good, then, or she wouldn't have been so good."

"Don't know about that. I've an idea that wicked folks do quite as much towards manufacturing saints as good ones. Expect I shall have great credit for the aid I've been to you in that direction, some time. Anyway, I can assure you that boys won't be very plenty about this house for a while to come."

To Katie the anticipation of the arrival meant

exchanging crochet-needle and worsted for dust-brush and broom; for grandpa Sears must have a room down stairs, and a bed in it, and an open fire, and brown rolls for tea, and pies with light crust, and all the other little alterations in family arrangements which form the "rights" of invalids and old people.

"How long is he going to stay?" asked Kate, before she had been at work half an hour.

"Always, if he likes."

Katie's dust-brush did not move the faster for this announcement. The prospect of giving up her studies for a few weeks for the sake of an old man whom she never saw, and who wouldn't care a straw for her, or the heathen, or anybody but himself, was bad enough; but to have it *always* — Katie was startled to notice how often her mind turned to the thought that people do not often live long after they are eighty-eight. The children caught her spirit, and moved about gloomily, as if expecting every moment that the next they would be packed into drawers and band-boxes, to be "out of the way while grandpa is here." Altogether, it was a dismal day; and Katie lay down at night dissatisfied.

Grandpa had come; but he had gone at once

to his room. Katie had not seen him, and did not wish to see him.

The next day she felt better, and went cheerfully about her work, though the house did seem wholly different from the one she worked in two days before. Grandpa was weary with his journey, and confined to his room. Mrs. Bancroft confined herself with him, except when she left to give some order for his comfort. Minnie and Edith crept about like little mice. The boys took lunch in a basket, and disappeared immediately after breakfast.

The second day was a repetition of the first. Even Walter gave a deliberate "Hurrah!" when, on the third, Ida told him the missionaries were to be brought out again in the evening. He took it as a sign that things were coming back to their normal state.

"Of course something'll happen to prevent it, though," he added. But nothing did happen; and early in the evening Mrs. Bancroft began:—

"Four centuries and a half of Mohammedan rule, nearly two of real, and as many more of mimic Mogul government, two centuries of Catholic missionary labor and commercial intercourse with all the leading nations of the world, had made no real impression on either the morals or the religion of the Hindoos; when, near the close of the last century, William Carey, a young English shoemaker, and licensed preacher, pasted up in his shop a map of the world, entered on it all the information he could gain as to the population, character, and religion of its countries, and looked up from his last to plan the beginnings of the work of modern missions.

"He spoke his thoughts to his father, and received for answer the question, 'William, are you mad?' He presented it at a ministers' meeting; and the chairman, Mr. Ryland, sprang frowning to his feet, and thundered out, 'Young man, sit down! When God means to convert the heathen, he will do it without your aid or mine.' He conversed, printed, and preached upon the subject, introducing it with never-failing patience wherever he had opportunity, at the same time giving all his busy moments — he had no leisure ones — to fitting himself for the work before him; and at last had the satisfaction of aiding in the organization of the Particular Baptist Society for Propagating the Gospel among the Heathen.

"Soon another was found who wished to go to India as a missionary, Rev. Mr. Thomas, who had been acting as surgeon in Bengal. At the meeting of the society Jan. 10, 1793, Mr. Carey and Mr. Thomas saw each other for the first time.

"'From Mr. Thomas's account,' said Mr. Fuller at that meeting, 'there is a gold-mine in India; but it seems almost as deep as the centre of the earth. Who will venture to explore it?'

"'I will go down,' said Mr. Carey; 'but remember that you must hold the ropes.'

"When we remember that Mr. Carey pledged himself to these extensive mining operations at a time when the entire capital of the society was little over thirteen pounds, and that even now it was not nearly sufficient to pay the passage-money, we can hardly wonder that his ministering brethren called him an enthusiast.

"At last, on the 10th of November, 1793, the missionaries set foot on 'the land of tigers and crocodiles.'"

"Did the tigers catch him?" asked Edith, who was growing restless for something more exciting in the story.

"Not *yet*, Edie; be patient," said Walter compassionately.

"Tigers are not so fond of missionaries as people are apt to think," said Mrs. Bancroft. "Calcutta, where Mr. Thomas settled, and commenced business as a surgeon, is a city of over four hundred thousand inhabitants; and tigers are not quite as plenty there as in New York. Mr. Carey fixed his home forty miles farther east, and only quarter of a mile from the *sunderbunds*, dense forests covering thousands of square miles in the delta of the Ganges, filled with tigers, jackals, leopards, and serpents; but the wild beasts feared his gun, and he had little trouble.

"Two hundred years earlier, Parliament had incorporated a trading company to do business in India. For nearly one hundred and fifty years this company went on its way, trading with the natives; employing weavers, and shipping the product of their looms to England; making fortunes for its stockholders and officers, and starving its subordinates; buying a little land as it needed it; and building petty forts to defend its warehouses, but with no more idea of ever governing India than the Liquor Dealers' Association of New York has of governing America, — perhaps with less.

"Previous to and during this time, one after another, Persia, Portugal, Holland, Denmark, and France had each coveted a slice of India and taken it, giving pay sometimes in money, but oftener in bullets.

"The next twenty years brought great changes; and in Carey's time this band of merchants, known as the East India Company, was the chief governing power in India."

"That must have been a great help to Carey," interposed Walter.

"Instead, it was his greatest hinderance. England had conquered India. Hindooism had conquered the English. In Carey's time, the morals of the English East-Indians were no better than those of the heathen. The officers of the East India Company kept sacred the feast of Durga, but paid no regard to the sabbath. They offered money to build an idol temple. They furnished Juggernaut with carpenters to repair his body, and servants to draw his car. They made offerings to the Ganges. Meanwhile Carey and Thomas were tolerated only because they reported themselves as indigo merchants, having accepted the offer of a Mr. Udney to take charge of two of his factories.

It was a common saying among the natives, that all tribes had some god, or form of worship: the English only were atheists. It was not a great mistake, so far as the officers of the East India Company were concerned. Their god was gold. They feared that education would make the Hindoos less manageable; they feared that preaching Christianity would excite them to riots. They had often run far greater risk of riot for the sake of gold: but gold was worth incurring risks for; and Christianity, to their minds, was not.

"For six years Carey and Thomas struggled with floods and drought and fever, native indifference, and English opposition; and then, when in 1799 new missionaries had arrived, they moved to Serampore, a Danish settlement of twenty acres, bought for a factory and trading-station two years before Clive began the conquest of India for Britain. Here the East India Company had no power, and could only watch the missionaries with the tender interest which a cat feels in a caged bird hung just beyond her reach. Here, in December, 1800, the first Hindoo convert was baptized, and, two years later, ordained. Here, six weeks after the baptism, the first edition of the Bengali New Testament was printed, followed within ten years by the entire Bible in Bengali, and New-Testament versions in seven other languages. Here, with untiring industry, Carey made the researches which led to the abolition of the yearly sacrifice of children at Gunga Sagor. Here he proved that he had talents of value even according to East India Company standards, and was called to be teacher of Sanscrit and Bengali in Fort William College in Calcutta. Here, with his two associates Marshman and Ward, he gathered a little native church. Around them clustered a band of missionaries; and by voice and press the news of the gospel went out for seventy miles around.

"Sometimes, for a little while, as Mr. Ward expressed it, missionaries were "tolerated like toads, instead of being hunted like wild beasts;" and then new stations were occupied, and converts gathered in them. Sometimes all public preaching was forbidden outside of the twenty acres of Danish territory.

"I wish I might tell you all the story of those years; but it is that you might understand another story, which is really not another, but a sequel, that I have told you this.

"Now let us cross the ocean to America. Here, in 1804, we find Adoniram Judson, a lad of sixteen, just entering college. He is a universal reader, a quick mathematician, brilliant in almost every department of study, and has but one ambition, — 'to be a great man.'

"Four years later he graduated, receiving the highest appointment. In the class above him was a brilliant young deist named E——. Partly through his influence, young Judson, too, became a deist, and remained so through his college-course.

"Some months after he graduated, while on a tour through New York, he stopped over night at a country inn. In the room next him, so the landlord told him, lay a sick and dying young man. Was he prepared? It seemed an absurd question for a deist to ask; and yet Judson asked it, or something asked it of him, all night long. Deism could deny the Bible-view of the future; but it could not assure him that for a change so great *no* preparation was needed. And yet he blushed at his anxiety for the stranger, and most of all at the thought, 'What would E—— say to all this?' It was a weary, terrible night.

"The next morning's sunshine brought a more cheerful frame of mind. He arose, and inquired for his fellow-lodger.

"'He is dead,' was the answer.

"'Dead?'

"'Yes, he is gone, poor fellow! The doctor said he could not survive the night.'

"'Do you know who it was?'

"'Oh, yes! It was a young man from Providence College, a fine fellow. His name was E——.'

"At first, Judson was stunned by the news. Then he was aroused to a new earnestness. He was a sceptic still, but from that day an honest and thoughtful one. In October, 1808, he entered Andover Theological Seminary, not as a candidate for the ministry, but as an inquirer for truth.. Soon he was a believer in Christ. In May, 1809, he united with the Third Congregational Church in Plymouth, of which his father was pastor. Almost at the same time he pledged himself to the work of foreign missions, never dreaming then that the voice that called him had spoken also to other ears.

"In the summer or fall of 1807, Samuel Mills, a student at Andover, asked Gordon Hall and

James Richards to take a walk with him; and there behind a haystack they spent a day in fasting and prayer, and talking about missions. That walk and talk resulted in a missionary society, whose records were kept in cipher, and whose members were pledged to secrecy, lest their Christian friends should laugh at their Quixotism.

"The kindred spirits soon met. Newell and Nott in Andover were, like Judson, interested in the work. Soon several members of the Williamstown society, among them Luther Rice, left Williamstown for Andover, and there the society was removed. The result of their earnestness was the organization of the American Board of Commissioners for Foreign Missions, which accepted the four students, Judson, Nott, Mills, and Newhall, as its missionaries. Luther Rice was afterwards added to the number, on condition that he raise funds for his own outfit and passage, which he did in six days. Judson, on the 5th of February, 1812, was married to Miss Ann Hasseltine. On the 19th, with Mr. and Mrs. Newell, they set sail for India, and in four months landed at Calcutta.

"Their arrival found the East India Company

in one of its worst and last spasms of missionary-phobia.

"Before the other missionaries who had sailed at nearly the same time with them had arrived, almost before they themselves had time to look around them, Judson and Newell were ordered back to America. They asked leave to go to some other part of India, but were refused. At last they gained leave to go, instead, to the Isle of France, hundreds of miles away, off the coast of Africa. There was but one ship about to sail for that port, and that had only room for Mr. and Mrs. Newell. The Judsons waited for another vessel, and for the arrival of 'The Harmony,' with the rest of the missionaries.

"They were American citizens, destined for Burmah. War had been declared between England and America. There were grave mutterings between England and Burmah. To be on English soil at this time, under any circumstances, was not pleasant: to be there in a capacity which would render even an English citizen liable to expulsion, was decidedly unpleasant. It was in this hour of isolation that they, with their own hand, cut the tie that bound them to their only human source of support, — the American Board.

"While they were crossing the ocean, Mr. Judson commenced studying the subject of baptism, partly that he might be ready to meet the arguments of the Baptist missionaries whose guest he expected to be at Serampore; partly that he might certainly know what to do with the children and servants of the converts from heathenism; whom his faith already saw as real beings.

"It was a needless labor so far as the Serampore missionaries were concerned, as no word was said to him on the subject, until, as the result of his investigations, he wrote a note requesting baptism. Mr. and Mrs. Judson were baptized by Mr. Ward, Sept. 6. Luther Rice had pursued similar studies on board 'The Harmony.'"

"I always said I had a hand in that business," interrupted grandpa Sears. Through the evening the old man had sat immovable, and the young people supposed asleep. Had the old mahogany sofa spoken, and declared that it had a hand in the missionary work, they could hardly have been more surprised.

"Tell us about it, grandfather," said Mrs. Bancroft.

"Baptists weren't very plenty in our region then. I was one; but I always went to church with the standing order. Well, somehow I'd got waked up about missions, like the rest of them; and, when Judson and Newell and those went out, I felt just like doing something. 'But then,' said I (or maybe 'twas the Tempter speaking to me), 'I don't know. They won't teach what you believe. Now, what's the use of your paying money to send out missionaries to teach things you don't believe?' I waited, and thought about it: and by and by I made up my mind that I couldn't help giving, anyway.; so I just gave, and just asked the Lord to see to it that somehow it all went to building up his own truth."

"And so, when the news came that Judson and Rice had turned Baptists, you thought your prayer was answered," said Clarence with an incredulous smile, which grandpa could not see.

"Yes, I did; not but other folks had prayed too, and not but 'twould have been answered somehow if that hadn't happened. Anyway, I was satisfied. And when I read in the next Board Report, 'A new cloud has been cast upon the affairs of the mission,' I thought, 'That

Board'll see the silver lining of the cloud some time;' and I guess it did. Twenty years after, its secretary wrote to Dr. Judson, 'We rejoice in the very great good that has grown out of your change of relation. We would not have it otherwise.' Nothing in the world would have waked up the Baptists as that did; and then, when Luther Rice came over— But I mustn't get ahead of our story.—Go on, mother."

"Before this 'The Harmony,' with the other missionaries, had come. Luther Rice too, as the result of his studies on the voyage, had become a Baptist. This was a great encouragement to Judson.

"But very soon there came an order that all the missionaries must sail for England in a ship then under way. Passage was engaged for them in the gunner's mess. How their wives were to be disposed of, they were not informed. Messrs. Hall and Nott escaped the notice of the police, and went to Bombay. Mr. and Mrs. Judson already had leave to go to the Isle of France, and applied for a pass. To their surprise, this was refused; but a vessel was ready to sail for that port, and, with Mr. Rice, they asked of its commander leave to go on board.

"'I will be neutral. There is the ship: you can do as you please,' was his reply.

"They went on board; but, when only fifteen miles below Calcutta, the ship was stopped, and forbidden to proceed with them. They landed, and went down the river to a hotel at Fultah. In vain they urged the captain of a vessel lying there to take them to Ceylon. No captain dared receive them. Yet to remain where they were was dangerous, and to go back to Calcutta even more so. Now, in the midst of their greatest distress, came the asked-for but refused pass.

"The vessel on which they started had been providentially detained some miles below. By rowing a night and a day, they reached it just as it was weighing anchor for the last time. On the 17th of January, they joined Mr. Newell at the Isle of France, — Mr. Newell only; for Mrs. Newell had died seven weeks before.

"A few months' stay convinced them that their work could make no progress while they remained there. It was decided that Mr. Rice should go back to America to arouse an interest in missions among the Baptists. He left on the 15th of March; and on the 7th of May the

Judsons embarked for Madras, entering again the lion's jaws with only the hope that they might have a chance to escape before he would have time to close them together.

"Information of the dangerous arrival was sent to the governor-general. How he would reply, they well knew. Their only hope was to be absent when his message came. The only vessel ready to sail was a rickety affair, bound for Rangoon in Burmah: on it they embarked. The voyage across the Bay of Bengal was a dreary one. Mrs. Judson was sick, so very sick, that, at one time, her husband could only look forward to being left wholly alone. Then they were driven into a dangerous strait, whose black rocks, half hidden beneath the waves, plainly told them they might have to choose between drowning and being cast on shore and eaten by savages. But the water of the strait was still, and Mrs. Judson grew better. They passed the rocks in safety, and favoring winds wafted them to Rangoon."

Mrs. Bancroft's little congregation dispersed. She was sitting alone for the evening, as she supposed, when Katie's light step descended the stairs, and she stood beside her.

"Mother."

"Well, Katie."

"Do you suppose I could borrow a geography and history? And could I use Walter's old grammar and arithmetic and book-keeping?"

"Why, Katie, what new spirit has possessed you?" asked Mrs. Bancroft, too much pleased to even laugh at Katie's extended plans.

"Nothing new. But Carey couldn't have learned languages so easily if he hadn't known something about grammar; and it was geography that made him a missionary partly, and — Mother, I believe one needs to know *every thing* to be a good missionary."

"You can have the books, certainly; but how will you find time for all this, Katie?"

Katie blushed; for "I haven't time" had been one of her stereotyped excuses.

"I read three novels, and crocheted a tidy, last month. I can do my sewing while you are talking in the evening; and I can give up my walks, if necessary."

"If you have really consecrated yourself — your health, strength, and all — to God, you must preserve them for his work: so I shall not let you give up your walks. You shall have all the books you need, and all the help I can give you."

The next morning, when the morning's work was done, Ida was surprised to find a slate-pencil instead of a crochet-needle between Katie's fingers.

CHAPTER IV.

JUDSON AND BURMAH.

IT is often easier to yield up our whole future lives to God than to give him the present moment. Many give up every thing for Christ's cause in their prayers, who hesitate when asked to give up some one thing in their practice.

Katie knew something about this one morning the next week, when, for the first time, she had gathered all her books around her, arranged her desk to suit her, and had nothing else to do but to study. It was really as much a part of Christ's work as if her grammar had been Sanscrit, or the figures which looked up discouragingly from her slate had been the inquiring faces of Hindoos or Burmans. Indeed, these studies were a part of the greater work she had planned so often, or she would not have undertaken them; but dreaming is easier than figuring, and Katie had practised the former to perfection, while she had quite neglected the latter.

She persevered patiently, until she came to one of those sums which neither patience nor perseverance can conquer, unless aided by natural mathematical talent; and Katie had none of this to aid her,—none in her own brain, at least; and there was not much comfort in knowing that there was plenty of it in a head just visible in the next room, bending over a comic almanac.

The almanac was thrown aside in a few minutes; and Walter passed through the dining-room, pausing at Katie's desk.

"What's up now?"

"Noth"— Katie did not finish the word. Truthfulness (which was natural to her) and humility (for which she had prayed) were struggling with pride.

It is a very easy thing, usually, to sacrifice selfishness on the altar of pride. If Katie had been asked to help Walter, she would have done it, and enjoyed doing it, and perhaps congratulated herself on the Christian spirit this showed; but receiving a favor from him was another affair. Yet she had prayed earnestly, the night before, that her spirit might be made like that humble, fervent spirit of which she had just heard, and that she might bow all her own private feelings to the work before her.

Truthfulness conquered in a moment.

"Here is a sum I can't do," she answered just as Walter was turning away. "I don't see how anybody can tell what was lost by the wreck of a ship, without knowing how much she was worth to begin with."

"I do," said Walter, glancing at the book, seizing the slate, and moving the pencil rapidly over it. In a few moments the work was done, the slate left on her desk, and Walter was out of the room.

"Yes, Walter could do it as easily as nothing, and I could not do it at all; and I suppose he despises me for it," Katie said to herself, never dreaming that Walter was at that moment thinking, that, in receiving the favor from him, Katie had done something he could not, and that, on the whole, he admired her for it.

While Walter was figuring for Katie, Ida passed through the room, looked toward them, but said nothing.

"Katie is really growing more practical, in spite of spending her evenings in India," she remarked afterwards to her sister.

"Say, rather, *because* of it," Mrs. Bancroft replied.

And Ida gave no answer, but, when evening came, herself called the children together to listen while Mrs. Bancroft continued the story:—

"You remember, on the map of the Eastern hemisphere, how the Bay of Bengal juts up into the southern coast of Asia, making it look as if it was bordered with badly made tape-trimming. At the head of the bay is Bengal; on its east coast, Orissa and Madras; on its western side, Burmah.

"Beautiful with rocks and valleys and mountain-ranges, with flowers and palms and banyans, rich in metals and gems and fruits and costly woods, abounding still more in the treasures sought by scientific students, in the raw material of geology, botany, and ethnology, Burmah has seemed for centuries to offer a perpetual card of invitation to the world; yet she has had few visitors, and to-day has hardly an intimate acquaintance.

"In her temples, no Brahmans trample upon

human souls. No caste, compelling even the kind-hearted to be cruel, distorts her society. Her sacred rivers roll innocently to the sea. Her hills, glistening with white pagodas, bear no blood-stains. A few plantain-leaves or a little fruit may be offered to Gaudama; but he is better served by acts of kindness, and gifts to the needy. In her cities, Chinese, Burmans, Talings, and Malays dwell together as peaceably, at least, as they would in America. No drunkards stagger in her streets. No oaths defile her air."

"Pardon the interruption; but it strikes me it would hardly be amiss for her to send missionaries to America," suggested Clarence. "Burmah must be the paradise of the world."

"No doubt Dr. and Mrs. Judson were greatly improved by the society they found there," said Walter gravely.

"Negatives, however multiplied, cannot make a paradise," replied Mrs. Bancroft. "The Burmans are Buddhists. But, whatever we may think of the Buddha who died in Hindostan twenty-four centuries ago, we cannot afford to spare much reverence for the Budda now worshipped under the name of Gaudama in Burmah,— a being innumerable leagues in height, who, a moment after his birth, called out with the voice of a lion, 'I am chief of the world!' who, at five months, sat on the air without support, split a hair with his arrow at the distance of ten miles, and, if it suited him, tumbled mountains and islands around promiscuously, and shook ten thousand worlds, merely for the fun of the thing. He passed, in all, through 25,600,000 transmigrations. It is as certain that he was a fox as that he was a man. The very place where he scratched as a cock can be shown. In his last state he remembered all that happened in the previous ones. He has entered Nigban now, where he is free alike from pain and pleasure, where 'there is neither being nor nothing.' But there is to be another Buddha: there may be many others. And somewhere, in some shape, all the Buddhas that are to be are in the universe now; no one can tell where: so all life, whether of man, tiger, or mosquito, is sacred. And there are priests who will not sit down without first carefully brushing their seat, lest they might accidentally crush some insect; for who could tell but the meanest worm might contain the soul of some future Buddha?

"The masses could not be expected to be as careful, however; and, since none of them could reasonably expect to go through life without being the means of some scores of murders, many do not hesitate to add to the list. Fishermen, and even butchers, are found among them. The superannuated horse was not often killed; but he was left to starve. The sacred ox might be inhumanly beaten; and men convicted of theft or robbery, or even less crimes, might lose hands or eyes or ears in the most barbarous manner possible.

"Even the gifts to the poor, and the deeds of kindness, which make a part of their religion, are done merely as acts of merit, and are usually received without gratitude. Or perhaps the recipient thinks he does his benefactor a favor in allowing him thus to add to his treasures in the next world. Robberies are common; though perhaps not more so than they would be here, if our houses were equally easy of access. Divorces are obtained as easily as our most advanced reformers would wish, and society suffers accordingly. Gambling and lying are almost universal.

"Schools are common: but you would laugh if you could see one, or rather before you saw it; for, long before you reached the schoolhouse, you might hear the yellow-robed priest calling off letters or words from the blackboard, and the whole school repeating after him in concert. In this way, it would take a child about three years to learn to read. Yet almost every one learns: it would be hard to tell why; for, when the missionaries came, young Burmah had hardly any thing to read except public documents, considerably less interesting to him than Acts of Congress would be to young America.

"They have a Bible, the Tripitika"—

"Tell me about it, if you please, madam," interrupted Clarence. "I am about undertaking a course of reading; and I thought I should commence with the Bibles of the world, and take the sacred books of the Buddhists first."

"Shall you read them 'on your bended knees,' as Mr. Emerson directs?" inquired Walter, guessing where Clarence borrowed his idea of a course of reading.

"You would bid fair to become as stiff as a Hindoo saint, if you did," said Mrs. Bancroft. "It is in several thousand volumes; and few of them have been translated. But I will read you a specimen from one: —

"'Om. Salutation to all Buddhas, Bodhisattvas, Aryas, Sravakas, and Pratyeka Buddhas of all times, past, present, and future, who are adored throughout the farthest limits of the ten quarters of the globe. Thus hath it been heard by me, that once on a time Bhajavat sojourned in the garden of Anathapindada, at Getavana in Sravasti, accompanied by a venerable body of twelve thousand Bhikshukas. There likewise accompanied him thirty-two thousand Bodhisattvas, all linked together by unity of caste, and perfect in the virtues of Paramita, who had made their command over Bodhisattva knowledge a pastime, were illumined with the light of Bodhisattva dharanis, and were masters of the dharanis themselves; who were profound in their meditations, all submissive to the lord of Bodhisattvas, and possessed absolute control over samadhi, great in self-command, refulgent in Bodhisattva forbearance, and replete with the Bodhisattva element of perfection'"—

"Couldn't you wait till to-morrow for the rest, Clarence?" asked Walter.

"But it isn't *all* like that, is it?" said Kate.

"A great part of it. Among the Buddha's own words, however, are some things well worth repeating; for example:—

"'He who should conquer in battle ten times a hundred thousand were indeed a hero; but truly a greater hero is he who has but once conquered himself.'

"'Hide your good deeds, and confess before the world the sins you have committed.'

"'Let a man overcome anger by love, evil by good, the greedy by liberality, the liar by truth.'

"'As a solid rock is not shaken by the wind, wise people falter not amid blame and praise.'

"'Let us live happily, not hating those who hate us. Let us dwell free from hatred among men who hate.'

"Gaudama admitted the existence of the Brahman gods as spirits; and now these spirits, under the name of Nats, receive from the masses a sort of lower worship. It is thought, too, that men may at death become Nats.

"Theatres are common and greatly patronized in Burmah; and I have read translations of several plays acted there, in which the Nats figured as largely, and were treated with as little reverence, as the gauze or mirrored ghosts in a theatre in New York.

"After all, to most of the people, the Buddhist worship is only a ceremony which they do not understand, but vaguely hope will somehow do them good, — a sacrifice less to Gaudama than to the universal conscience.

"We left the Judsons just entering Burmah. Luther Rice had returned to America, and was going through the country, kindling a hitherto unknown missionary zeal among its churches; but of this no tidings reached Rangoon.

"For three long years Mr. and Mrs. Judson labored alone. For months, except now and then when a sea-captain called, they saw no European face, and heard their own language only from each other's lips. Together, alone, they celebrated the Lord's Supper. Around them tinkled the silvery bells of pagodas; before them passed the Buddhist monks, bearing their bowls for offerings. Now and then, along their path, a funeral-procession. wound its way, with sounds of gongs and trumpets. Women came, and felt curiously of Mrs. Judson's white hands, and handled her garments. Men gazed at the 'new white foreigner' as they would at a new white elephant, only with much less reverence. That was all. Day after day they worked at Burman crooks and circles under a teacher who knew no English, and could only tell them the Burman names of objects as they pointed at them. At first, he declined teaching Mrs. Judson; it was beneath his dignity to teach a woman: but Mr. Judson's wishes finally prevailed.

"As soon as the missionaries had learned the use of their tongues in the new language, they began to talk of Christ.

"'Your religion is good for you, and ours for us. You will be rewarded in your way, and we in ours,' came the answer.

"Then Mrs. Judson was taken sick, and had to go to Madras for three months to save her life. In August, 1815, a little baby came; but, after eight months, God took it again. Then, just as Mr. Judson had nearly finished a Burman tract and a grammar of the language, and had commenced translating the Gospel of Matthew, he was seized with severe pain in his head, and his eyes became so weak that crooks and circles melted together before him, and he could not even read his English Bible."

"I should have given up," said Charlie.

"At that very time he wrote to Luther Rice,

'If a ship were lying in the river, ready to carry me to any part of the world I should choose, and that with the entire approval of all my Christian friends, I would prefer dying to embarking.'

"And Mrs. Judson wrote, 'God grant that we may live and die among the Burmans, though we should never do any thing more than smooth the way for others.'

"In 1816 they received from Serampore a present of a printing-press, and from America a man to use it. Mr. and Mrs. Hough were the first missionaries sent out by the Baptist Missionary Convention. A tract, a grammar, and the first chapters of Matthew, had already been translated: so press and man found immediate employment, and soon the tracts were ready for distribution.

"One day in March, 1817, as Mr. Judson was sitting with his teacher, there came up the steps a respectable-looking Burman, followed by a servant.

"'Where do you come from?' asked Mr. Judson.

"The man gave no definite answer, but, before long, surprised the missionary by the question, 'How long time will it take me to learn the religion of Jesus?'

"'That question cannot be answered,' said Mr. Judson. 'If God gives light and wisdom, the religion of Jesus is soon learned; but, without God, a man might study his life long, and make no proficiency. But how came you to know any thing of Jesus? Have you ever been here before?'

"'No.'

"'Have you seen any writing concerning Jesus?'

"'I have seen two little books.'

"'Who is Jesus?'

"'He is the Son of God, who, pitying creatures, came into this world, and suffered death in their stead.'

"'Who is God?'

"'He is a being without beginning or end, who is not subject to old age and death, but always is.'

"Mr. Judson handed him a tract and catechism. He recognized them both, and read here and there in them, remarking to his follower, 'This is the true God; this is the right way.'

"Mr. Judson tried to talk with him; but he seemed only to care to get another book. Mr. Judson told him he had no other, but was busy translating one, which he should have before long.

"'But have you not a little of that book done which you will graciously give me now?' persisted the inquirer.

"So Judson folded and gave him the first five chapters of Matthew; and the man went away."

"Did he ever become a Christian?" asked Edith.

"I do not know that he did. Three weeks later, they heard that he read their books all day, and showed them to all who called on him. A year later they met him. He had been made ruler of a cluster of villages in Pegu. He still read the books, recommended the tract to his servants, and asked Mr. Judson to preach to his people. Probably, fear of persecution kept him back."

"A rather discouraging sign for the future," remarked Charlie.

"To one who knows he is doing God's work in God's way, all signs are signs of promise. This first inquirer proved that the Burman mind was not impenetrable, as it had seemed; and Mr. Judson saw in him a call for more workers."

"And we sent them two," interrupted grandpa. "I only wish you could have seen Coleman and Wheelock, — perfect gentlemen, and real workers. They began with the sailors as soon as they stepped on board ship; and six or seven were converted before they reached Calcutta. But Wheelock lived only one year, and Coleman two."

"What a pity they started!" said Clarence.

"I don't know. We're apt, when our friends die, to be glad if we've let them have what they wanted: and, if a man's hungry for missionary work, I don't know why he shouldn't be gratified just as much as if he's hungry for oranges; and Coleman and Wheelock were just that. They begged to be made missionaries as another man would beg to be made governor. 'I had rather be a missionary of the cross than a king on his throne,' Wheelock wrote; and Coleman, 'Never did a man famishing with hunger partake of food with more satisfaction than we beheld the shores of Burmah;' and Mrs. Wheelock added, 'Nothing would be more dreadful than the thought of returning to my native land.'"

"Well, tastes differ," said Clarence, taking advantage of one of those safe refuges that are open alike to all disputants.

"I was going to tell how Ward visited us, and then Mrs. Judson, and how we sent out Dr. Price; but I guess it's mother's turn now."

"Dr. Price — was he a D.D. when he started?" asked Walter with suddenly awakened interest.

"No, a medical man: such can do some things better than anybody else. Now, mother.".

"The first thing to be done after Coleman and Wheelock landed was to build a meeting-house, or, as they called it, a zayat. The first public worship was held there on the 4th of April, 1819. On the 25th, it was permanently opened for public instruction in religion; and for a week inquirers came and went as plentifully as, and with about the same spirit with which, inquirers would visit a Buddhist priest, should one set up a similar edifice by the wayside in New York or Philadelphia.

"It is late now. Next week we will spend a while with Judson in his new quarters."

"What's the matter with Walter?" said Katie after the circle had broken up. "He has hardly said a word all the evening."

"And what made him wake up so suddenly when grandpa spoke of Dr. Price?" asked Edith.

Because the mother's eye had caught something which awakened hopes she dared not express, she only gave the answer, — almost always a safe one, — "I don't know."

CHAPTER V.

THE FIRST BURMAN CHRISTIANS.

OW, Miss Ida, if I had about three yards of your strongest twine, I would finish my derrick."

Ida did not doubt the truth of Walter's statement; but, as she could not see that the world would be any the better for the completion of a five-foot derrick, she made no answer.

"Please?" said Charlie inquiringly.

"It is up stairs; and I am too busy to go for it."

"Let *us* go."

"You would disarrange things."

About two minutes' silence, and Charlie muttered, "Let's try Kate."

Kate sat with slate and pencil in hand. A few mornings of earnest work had done wonders in collecting and arranging the ideas that had been promiscuously scattered into her brain during her school-days; and, for the sake of her studies, she had very cheerfully accepted the interruption of the missionary talks for a few evenings. She was *very* busy when the boys burst in upon her.

"How's Sir Isaac to-day?" Sir Isaac was the most recent of the thousand and one names by which Walter designated Katie.

Katie's brow knit a little. She was afraid of losing track of her work.

"Could he come down from his calculations among the clouds to provide a forlorn derrick with something stronger than a mathematical line for a cord?"

"O Walter! I can't now" —

"Just imagine I'm a heathen, Kate; and then it'll come easy."

"I can easily imagine it," replied Kate; " but " —

"Then suppose you were a missionary, and could accommodate the heathen that way."

Katie went up stairs without a word, and returned with the cord. The last two evenings had convinced her that the missionary life was, after all, only doing daily among the heathen the very best and kindest and most Christian things one could. And why should she not do them here? If not, she could not there.

Walter entered the sitting-room, making a long flourish over Ida's head with his cord.

"If I had nothing nearer than India to occupy my mind, I could afford to be as obliging as Katie," Ida replied a little tartly. "I hope to make *my* life of some practical use."

"What have you got to do now?" asked Charlie.

"What have you got to do?" was a question Ida was always ready to answer.

"First I must finish an apron for Mrs. Keith's baby; then I must make some broth for Widow Lane; then I told Mr. Parsons I would make arrangements for the Sunday-school meeting (poor man, the people take hold so poorly, he is almost discouraged); then I have two flounces to bind, and a watch-case to finish; then Minnie must have her primer lesson" —

"Now, Ida, I'm going to give you a piece of my mind," interrupted Walter. "Of course, nobody but a heathen would hint that flounces and watch-cases aren't practical; but I do protest, that if it's sensible to make a bear of yourself for the sake of Sunday schools, and discouraged ministers, and primer lessons, here, it's just as much so to do it for the same things in India; and that saving babies from the alligators, and widows from the fire, is just as practical business as making aprons and broth for them."

"They don't burn widows and kill babies now," said Ida.

"Maybe not. They would, though, if everybody had always been as *practical* as you are."

The door closed.

Quarrelling is wicked; but if people would always go away after it, and think over what has been said, it might be made quite useful. "Is my life a practical one, after all?" was the question which this quarrel forced upon Ida; and she thought about it at intervals, until in the evening she joined the group gathered to listen to the story:—

"On the 1st of May, out of the crowd that were flocking past to the great pagoda at the end of the road, there came into the zayat a young man called Moung Nau. He had come the day before, but was too silent and reserved to be counted as an inquirer. Inquirers, or rather questioners, were plenty that day; for it was Burman worship day, and some of them excited strong hope. But on the next Sunday only one of them all was found in the little company of thirty that gathered to hear Mr. Judson preach; and that one was Moung Nau. Most of the audience were restless and thoughtless: he was quiet and attentive. Day after day, he came steadily; while others came, satisfied their curiosity about the strange teacher, and went away, not to return.

"At last Mr. Judson began to hope that Moung Nau was really a Christian. 'It seems almost too much to believe that God has begun to manifest his grace to the Burmans,' he writes in his journal of May 5; 'but this day I could not resist the delightful conviction that this is indeed the case. PRAISE AND GLORY BE TO HIS NAME FOREVERMORE. AMEN.'

"On May 8 he writes, 'Burman day of worship. Thronged with visitors through the day. Moung Nau was with me a great part of the day, and assisted me much in explaining things to new-comers.'

"MAY 9.—'Only two or three of all I conversed with yesterday came again. Had, however, an assembly of thirty. In the course of conversation, Moung Nau declared himself a disciple of Christ in the presence of a considerable number.'

"MAY 11. — 'Heard much to-day of the danger of introducing a new religion. Those who seemed most favorably disposed whispered me that I had better not stay in Rangoon and talk to the common people, but go directly to the "Lord of life and death." If he approved of the religion, it would spread rapidly; but, in the present state of things, nobody would dare to prosecute inquiries.'

"MAY 15. — 'Moung Nau has been with me all day, as well as yesterday. He is anxious to be received into our company, and thinks it a great privilege to be the first among the Burmans in professing the religion of Christ.'

"On the 6th of June he sent to the missionaries, of his own accord, a letter, telling of his faith in Christ, giving a clear view of the Christian religion, and asking baptism.

"Two weeks later, before the sleepy eyes of a stone Gaudama who kept guard over the artificial pond near by, the first Burman convert was baptized.

"Perhaps it was well for the early Burman converts that the god they had worshipped had always been entirely indifferent to the question whether he was worshipped or not.

"But, though Gaudama would never trouble himself about their defection, there stood always before them the nearer terror, — the viceroy, the woongyee, the emperor; for this thing must some time reach the golden ears; and what right had a subject, a slave, to think differently from the 'Lord of heaven and earth'? Then there were stories of a sect of Buddhists that had been suppressed by the sword; of a Catholic convert beaten till his body was one livid wound: and filling the air around them were the Nats, wild, roving spirits, true descendants of the discrowned Brahman gods; there was no telling what uncanny things they might do. So it was not a light thing for the poor young workman, Moung Nau, to stand alone, a Christian in a nation of Buddhists, following that other poor young workman, who, eighteen hundred years before, stood alone in Palestine.

"Meanwhile 'the immortal king, wearied with the fatigues of royalty, had gone up to amuse himself in the celestial regions,' or, in plain

English (it would have been a crime to hint the thing in Burman), had died. His body had been burned on a pile of perfumed wood anointed with costly oils; his ashes collected in an urn, and buried in the royal cemetery; his grandson seated on his throne; his brother and other troublesome relatives tucked into red sacks, and respectfully drowned; and the empire was running on as before.

"Inquirers came and went; hopes rose and fell. Sometimes the little zayat would be crowded; sometimes almost deserted. Often Burmans would come for days in succession, and appear fully convinced of the truth of Christianity, when some rumor of probable persecution would drive them away, not to return. Sometimes one who appeared to be an inquirer would turn out to be a Buddhist priest, or a bitter reviler of religion. Often a listener, convinced, but not converted, would turn away with the remark, 'Superior wisdom compels me to bow;' and there his inquiries would end.

"But there were some who showed they had begun to feel that hunger for which Buddhism offers no food. Among these were Moung Byaa, Moung Thalah, Moung Ing, and Moung

Shwa-gnong. Moung Thalah was an interesting young man, a quick thinker, and ready talker. Moung Byaa was a member of Mrs. Judson's school. These two were soon received into the church; and Mr. Judson writes:—

"Nov. 14.—'Lord's Day. Have been much gratified to find that this evening the three converts repaired to the zayat, and held a prayer-meeting of their own accord.'

"Buddhism was not all that Judson had to contend with. Atheism, like pauperism and idiocy, is found everywhere. Types of religion, like forms of wealth and learning, vary, and make men vary; but the absolutely lacking are essentially the same in Burmah and in Boston. Why this fact should furnish ground of boasting, I am unable to see; but in Burmah, at least, there is no prouder set of men than those who have abjured the gods their neighbors worship, and taken nothing in their place. Judson found no bitterer opponents. Having no lines of belief to defend, they had the same advantage in discussion that the guerilla has over the ordinary soldier in warfare. All the arguments directed against idolatry were powerless against them. The Buddha was to them only a man; Buddhism, a useful lie. They believed in the eternity of wisdom, but not in a being eternally wise. Beyond this, they believed nothing; and generally their belief in the eternal wisdom did not prevent their following the dictates of temporal wisdom, so far as to bow before pagodas, and make offerings to Gaudama.

"A leader and teacher in one of these sects was Moung Shwa-gnong. He first came to the zayat Aug. 26, 1819. Tall, strong mentally and physically, a man of commanding influence, and a frequent visitor, I suspect his image haunted Mr. Judson's dreams by night, and his thoughts by day, for some time afterward. 'Oh that he may be brought in!' Mr. Judson writes Sept. 19, 'if it be not too great a favor for this infant mission to receive.'

"At first he seemed to argue rather with the idea of silencing or converting Mr. Judson than of being converted by him; but in time he grew more seriously interested. Finally he admitted the existence of an eternal God.

"Then there spread through the Buddhist ranks, and reached those ears that were hearing-trumpets for the golden ears, a whisper that Moung Shwa-gnong was going over to the foreign religion. 'Inquire further,' said the viceroy; and the words sent terror to the hearts of Christians and inquirers, and especially of Moung Shwa-gnong. He went to the Mangen teacher who had accused him, and apologized and explained and flattered, and somehow satisfied him.

"Meanwhile a poor fisherman, Moung Ing, joined the circle of inquirers, and before long professed himself a believer. 'Thus,' writes Mr. Judson, 'the poor fisherman Moung Ing is taken, and the learned teacher Moung Shwa-gnong left.'

"Moung Shwa-gnong called soon after; but his call was short and formal. The rest deserted the zayat entirely. Mr. Judson sat there for days together without a single visitor. Curiosity-hunters no longer wished to come; inquirers dared not. One morning, as Mr. Judson took his usual ride through the grounds of the great pagoda, he was met by the Mangen teacher, with an order from the viceroy that he must ride there no more under pain of being beaten, — a circumstance trifling in itself, but important as a straw showing the state of the wind.

"Aside from the abandonment of the work

(which they did not even think of), but one course seemed to open before the missionaries, — they must go themselves to the capital, and present their cause to the emperor.

"Before they left, they received another visit from Moung Shwa-gnong. Hours passed in discussing his deistical cavils; but finally he owned that he did not believe any thing he had said, but had been merely trying the strength of Mr. Judson and his religion.

"Later in the day, when he and the missionary were alone, he said, 'This day is different from all the days on which I have visited you. I see now my error in trusting in my own reason. I now believe in the crucifixion of Christ (a point concerning which he had been especially incredulous), because it is contained in the Scripture.'

"Some time after, he said, 'I think I should not be lost, though I should die suddenly.'

"'Why not?' asked Mr. Judson.

"'Because I love Christ.'

"'Do you really love him?'

"'No one that knows him can help loving him.'

"And so he departed.

"They saw little more of him till just as they

were pushing off from Rangoon, when they caught a glimpse of his tall form standing on the wharf, waving them adieu with his hand.

"Up the Irrawadi, for a full month, the missionaries sailed, with the hope, that if they could reach Ava, present themselves at the golden feet, and gain audience of the golden ears, they could secure religious toleration. They saw the king; but their hopes were wholly disappointed. God did not mean that his infant cause in Burmah should be rocked by royal fingers.

"'In regard to the objects of your petition, his Majesty gives no order; in regard to your sacred books, his Majesty has no use for them; take them away,' was their final answer; and they went out of the palace with much less hinderance than they had entered it.

"They were far worse off than if they had not come. Their defeat would be known at Rangoon; and, if people had feared to inquire when royal protection was merely doubtful, what could be expected now that it was definitely withheld?

"At Pyee, two hundred and thirty miles from the capital, they met Moung Shwa-gnong, on a visit to an old acquaintance dangerously ill. Mr. Judson told him every thing, — the repulse at court, the entire failure of the expedition, the certainty that persecution lay before them; and closed with the story of the Catholic convert, years before, beaten almost to death with the iron mall.

"Moung Shwa-gnong was not frightened: on the contrary, he expressed himself rather too bravely for the circumstances.

"'It is not for you that we are concerned,' said Mr. Judson, 'but for those who have professed Christ. When they are accused, they cannot worship at the pagodas, nor recant before the Mangen teacher.'

"Moung Shwa-gnong felt the force of this reflection, and tried to explain.

"'Say nothing,' said Mr. Judson. 'One thing you know, that, when formerly accused, if you had not in some way or other satisfied the mind of the Mangen teacher, your life would not now be remaining in your body.'

"'Then,' said he, 'if I must die, I shall die in a good cause. I know it is the cause of truth. I believe,' he added emphatically, 'in the eternal God, in his Son Jesus Christ, in the atonement which Christ has made, and in the writings of the apostles as the true and only word of God.

Perhaps you may not remember, that, during my last visits, you told me I was trusting in my own reason rather than in the word of God. Since then I have seen my error, and endeavored to renounce it. You explained to me, also, the evil of worshipping at pagodas, though I told you my heart did not partake in the worship. Since you left Rangoon, I have not lifted up my folded hands before a pagoda. Now you say that I am not a disciple. What lack I yet?'

" 'Teacher,' replied Mr. Judson, 'you may be a disciple at heart; but you are not a full disciple. You have not faith and resolution enough to keep all the commands of Christ, particularly that which requires you to be baptized, though in the face of persecution and death.'

"Moung Shwa-gnong heard this in silence. He evidently had something to think about. Soon after, Mr. Judson hinted that the missionaries might be obliged to leave Rangoon.

"This roused him. 'Say not so,' he said. 'There are some who will investigate, notwithstanding; and, rather than have you quit Rangoon, I will go myself to the Mangen teacher, and have a public dispute with him. I know the truth is on my side.'

"'Ah!' said Mr. Judson, 'you may have a tongue to silence him; but he has a pair of fetters and an iron mall to tame you. Remember that.'

"Mr. Judson belonged to that small number of men to whom telling the exact truth is a necessity. This made him seem sometimes harsh, even severe; but perhaps this very severity, which so often marks his dealings with inquirers, saved the early Burman church from those distressing cases of discipline which are the saddest and most frequent trial alike of missionaries and pastors.

"A wakeful night followed this talk with Moung Shwa-gnong. Could they leave to eternal darkness souls already asking for light? On the other hand, could they stand by and encourage their disciples in the face of infernal tortures, and even of death? Might not their own flesh fail when their turn came to endure them? And could they hope, that, when the result of the visit to the palace was known, even one of the three baptized would remain firm? About these subjects they talked till midnight, and thought till nearly morning.

"They reached Rangoon on Friday. On Sunday they called the three disciples together, and gave them a full account of the affair. To the joy of the missionaries, instead of being intimidated, they vied with each other in expressing their love to Christ, and devotion to his cause.

"' But whither are the teachers going?' they asked, when Mr. Judson spoke of leaving Rangoon.

"Mr. Judson told them of Chittagong, where the death of an English missionary had left a band of native Christians as sheep without a shepherd. It was there that the teachers meant to go.

"'And what will *you* do?' they asked the disciples.

"Moung Nau had already said he should follow them to any part of the world.

"'As for me, I go where preaching is to be had,' said Moung Thahla.

"Moung Byaa was silent. He was married; and no Burman woman could be allowed to leave the country.

"' But if I must be left here alone,' he said at last, 'I shall remain performing the duties of Jesus Christ's religion. No other shall I think of.'

"A few days later he came with his brother-in-low, Moung Myatyah, an inquirer.

"'Teacher,' said Moung Byaa, 'my mind is distressed. I can neither eat nor sleep since I find you are going away. I have been around among those who live near us; and I find some who are even now examining the new religion. Do stay with us a few months. Stay till there are eight or ten disciples; then appoint one to be the teacher of the rest. I shall not be concerned about the event. The religion will spread of itself. The emperor cannot stop it.'

"In the same way spoke the rest. Soon fresh inquirers made the path of duty plain. Yet Chittagong ought not to be neglected: so Mr. and Mrs. Coleman went there, while the Judsons remained at Rangoon.

"And now Moung Shwa-gnong commenced the sober business of undoing the work of his past life. 'I know nothing,' he would say to those who had looked up to him as infallible. 'If you want true wisdom, go to the foreign teacher, and you will find it.'

"He gave this advice to Mah Menla, a woman, who, in mind, was among Burman women what Moung Shwa-gnong himself was among men.

Two years before, she had met with a tract which gave her some idea of an eternal God. Before long she joyfully received Christ. 'I am surprised,' she said, 'to find this religion has such an effect upon my mind as to make me love Christ more than my dearest natural relatives.'

"Before July 17, five more had been baptized, among them Moung Shwa-ba, who soon felt called to preach; but Moung Shwa-gnong and Mah Menla were not among them, and Moung Shwa-gnong had for some time been missing from the zayat.

"And now Mrs. Judson's illness compelled a voyage to Calcutta. Just before they started, the teacher made his appearance. Mr. Judson received him with some reserve, but soon found he had staid away from illness, not from choice. Before evening, others came in; and, as if to bring things to a crisis, Moung Shwa-gnong said, ' My lord teacher, there are now several of us present who have long considered this religion. I hope that we are all disciples of Christ.'

"'I am afraid to say that,' replied Mr. Judson: 'however, it is easily ascertained; and let me begin with you, teacher. I have heretofore thought that you fully believed in the eternal God; but I have had some doubt whether you fully believed in the Son of God and the atonement which he has made.'

"'I assure you,' Moung Shwa-gnong replied, 'that I am as fully persuaded of the latter as of the former.'

"'Do you believe, then, that none but the disciples of Christ will be saved from sin and hell?'

"'None but his disciples.'

"'How, then, can you remain without taking the oath of allegiance to Jesus Christ, and becoming his full disciple in body and soul?'

"'It is my earnest desire to do so by receiving baptism; and for the very purpose of expressing that desire I have come here to-day.'

"'You say you are desirous of receiving baptism: may I ask *when* you desire to receive it?'

"'At any time you will please to give it. Now, this moment, if you please.'

"'Do you wish to receive baptism in public, or in private?'

"'I will receive it at any time, and under any circumstances you may please to direct.'

"'Teacher,' said Mr. Judson, 'I am satisfied, from your conversation this forenoon, that you are a true disciple; and I reply, therefore, that I am as desirous of giving you baptism as you are of receiving it.'

"Mr. Judson then questioned Moung Thahla.

"'If the teacher, Moung Shwa-gnong, consents,' he said, 'why should I hesitate?'

"'And, if he does not consent, what then?'

"'I must wait a little longer.'

"'Stand by,' said Mr. Judson. 'You trust in Moung Shwa-gnong rather than in Jesus Christ. You are not worthy of being baptized.'

"The other men were still farther from committing themselves. Mah Menla said with some hesitation, that she desired baptism, if Mr. Judson thought it suitable. But Mr. Judson replied that he could not baptize any one who could possibly remain easy without.

"Moung Shwa-gnong was joyfully received by the church; and a day later, just at night, he was baptized.

"'Ah! he has gone to obey the command of Christ, while I remain without obeying. I shall not be able to sleep to-night. I must go home and consult my husband, and return.'

"About nine o'clock she returned, and requested baptism. Late at night, by lantern-light, Mr. Judson led her out to a pond near the house, and baptized her.

"The next day the Judsons embarked for Calcutta. On their return, more than five months later, they found every convert firm, and rejoicing to see them.

"Moung Shwa-gnong was not disappointed in his expectation of persecution. Up to the time of his baptism, his acquaintances had not thought it a possible thing that the great teacher would allow himself to be put under water by a foreigner. When the fact was known, all the priests and officers of the village where he lived entered into a conspiracy to destroy him. They held daily consultations. At length one of them sounded the viceroy with the complaint, 'Moung Shwa-gnong is doing every thing in his power to turn the priests' rice-pot bottom upwards.'

"'What consequence?' answered the viceroy. 'Let the priests turn it back again;' and the hopes of the conspiracy were blasted.

"Soon the fisherman Moung Ing, the second convert, and Mah Myatlah, were added to the church.

"On the 21st of August, Mrs. Judson was compelled, by rapidly declining health, to leave Burmah for England and America. In December, Dr. Price arrived from America. Very soon the fame of his skill reached Ava, now the capital. All articles of especial value discovered in the Burman Empire are at once appropriated by the king. Dr. Price was sent for. There were now eighteen converts at Rangoon, all active workers. Mr. and Mrs. Hough could take care of the mission there till more help should arrive. Mr. Judson decided to accompany Dr. Price to Ava, and, if the apparent opening proved a real one, remain with him.

"It was not until the fourth day from their arrival, after he had had several conversations with Dr. Price, that his Majesty noticed Mr. Judson.

"'And you in black, what are you? A medical man, too?' he asked.

"'Not a medical man, but a teacher of religion, your Majesty.' The king made a few inquiries about the religion; and then asked the alarming question, 'Have any embraced it?'"

"'Not here.'

"'Are there any at Rangoon?'"

"'There are a few.'

"'Are they foreigners?'

"I think, from a passage in his journal, that, even to Mr. Judson's mind, there occurred the possibility of evading *this* question; but the temptation, if it came, left unharbored.

"'There are some foreigners and some Burmans,' he replied.

"The king was at first silent, but evidently not displeased; for he soon began again to ask questions on religion, geography, and astronomy.

"For three months Mr. Judson remained at Ava, now discussing natural sciences with the royal family, now laboring with court officials to gain permission to occupy a piece of land with a mission-house, but pressing the claims of God and religion upon his noble listeners as earnestly and fearlessly as he had pressed them upon the fishermen and lumberers of Rangoon.

"In January, 1823, he gained the desired permission, and sailed for Rangoon. In August he completed the translation of the New Testament, in the version of which he had been aided by Moung Shwa-gnong. In December he welcomed back Mrs. Judson.

"Mr. and Mrs. Wade sailed with her. A

week after they reached Rangoon, Mrs. Judson was packed with her husband and all her goods into a little boat, and sailing for Ava.

"On their way they met the Burman general, Bandula, with a fleet of war-boats ready to invade the British province of Chittagong, bearing with him, it was said, golden fetters with which to bind Lord Amherst, and orders, after taking Calcutta, to march on and capture London. This was only one of many affronts that 'the lord of land and water' had offered to the insignificant little island of Great Britain; and the insults had been received in a manner which the Burman king could explain in but one way, — the English were afraid of him. He was satisfied that it would not be a difficult thing for his invincible army to conquer British India, or even England itself.

"When the Judsons reached Ava, they found all interest concentrating upon the approaching war, Dr. Price no longer in favor, and a shadow of suspicion resting upon all foreign residents."

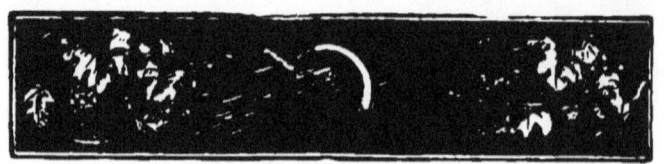

CHAPTER VI.

IN PRISON.

SECOND childhood is often as beautiful as first. When the world is thoroughly civilized and Christianized, I think we shall hear of the adoption of homeless old men into families as grandfathers, as we now hear of the adoption of infants as children and grandchildren; and people will watch the man who is ripening into an angel with the same interest and tenderness they now give the child who is ripening into a man.

Every thing has to make way for an old man as for a baby; but, in a well-regulated household, things are much more flexible than they are generally supposed to be. Grandpa Sears had not been in the house two weeks, before it was as natural to Katie to place his chair by the fire, and shake up his cushion, and comb his thick white hair, and dust his room, and in a thousand ways keep a half-motherly, half-daughterly watch over him, as to carry on her studies.

And in many ways grandpa Sears helped. The frequent spectacle and hat-and-cane hunts were excellent discipline for the children. The many ways in which even little Minnie had to yield her way to grandpa were teaching her unselfishness, very much as a new baby would have done; only there was no one to incur the risk the last baby always runs of being spoiled itself while endeavoring to educate other people. And then grandpa had lived when missions began; and the early missionary histories, which, in Katie's mind, had ranked with those of the crusades or the Reformation, grew real and present as she talked with him, and her missionary zeal kindled more than ever.

But missionary zeal was no longer a thing to be laid on the shelf for future use. "To do the best and kindest things I can to everybody here, or in India, or anywhere else," was a definition of the missionary work that was rapidly working its way into Katie's daily life. And it was surprising how much more interesting every thing around her became in consequence,— her Sunday-school class, her neighbors, Ida's pet widows and babies and sick people, the children of the family, everybody.

And, while Katie was learning that there were souls to save here as well as in India, Ida was beginning to see, that, as God looked at things, the importance of any particular field of labor did not depend upon the fact that she was in it, and that a work that would be practical where she lived might not be wholly visionary ten thousand miles away. She said little ; but that little signified so much, that it was no surprise, when on the next missionary evening, which came this time after three weeks' delay, she herself placed the chairs, and called the group together to listen to Mrs. Bancroft's story.

"We left Bandula on his way to Chittagong. The British soon heard of their approaching guest, and resolved to return the call before it was made. Suddenly a British fleet appeared before Rangoon. Orders were given by the Burman officers for the arrest, and, in case of firing, the immediate execution, of every man in Rangoon wearing a hat. Messrs. Hough and Wade were thrust, with others, into prison, where they waited the firing of the gun that should be their death-signal. The sand was spread that should drink their blood, and the guard were sharpening with bricks their weapons of death, when the attack began, and the first ball came flying directly over their heads. Others followed. Panic-struck, the guard fled, too anxious for their own lives to take those of their prisoners. Soon came a pause in the firing, and a moment of hope for the missionaries. Then fifty Burmans rushed in, seized the prisoners, bound them tightly with cords, drove them at the point of their spears to the place of execution, bent forward their bodies; and the spotted-faced executioner stood ready, waiting the word to strike. The command was given. Mr. Hough alone knew enough of the language to understand it. He turned, and begged the Yawoon to let him go to the British fleet and try to persuade them to stop firing. Then there came another shower of shot and shell, and the crowd, Yawoon and all, fled, driving the prisoners, still tightly chained, before them for a mile and a half. Their wives had passed a sleepless night at the mission-house, cheered only by the presence and prayers of Moung Shwa-ba, who remained with them. In the morning they went out; and now, disguised by blackened faces and Burman dress, they stood by the wayside, and saw their husbands driven past to die. When the fugitives halted, Mr. Hough renewed his petition. It was granted, but with the threat, that, if he failed to stop the firing, all the prisoners would be instantly killed. He went; but the firing did not cease. Through the night Mr. Wade lay on the ground, in a dungeon near the great pagoda, without food or drink, almost without clothing, his ankles galled with unwieldy iron chains, waiting hour by hour the summons to death. With the morning came the British troops. Rangoon was captured, and the prisoners released. Soon fever took up the work in which the Burmans had failed. Thousands of British soldiers fell victims. Mr. and Mrs. Wade were among the sufferers. As soon as they could endure the journey, they went with Mr. and Mrs. Hough to Bengal, where they remained till the close of the war."

"And where were the Judsons?" asked Edith.

"With Dr. Price at Ava. The news of the capture reached the capital in about two weeks. Suspicion at once fell upon all foreign residents. The missionaries were arrested with others as spies; and, within three months from their arrival, the men who had come to Ava by the royal invitation, were, by the royal command, strung upon a bamboo pole, manacled each with three pair of fetters, and thrust with seventy others into the darkest and filthiest of Burman prisons."

"But you can't think how often *we* asked, 'Where are the Judsons?'" interrupted grandfather. "How we watched and waited and waited, and almost fought for the first look at the magazine, and then dropped it, half uncut, when we found there was no news all those months after Mr. Hough wrote about the attack on Rangoon. You can't know any thing about it unless"— the old man looked at Mrs. Bancroft, and his voice grew softer — "you have watched for letters from some one in the army or on the sea that *never* came back. It was most like that."

"Now," resumed Mrs. Bancroft, "for twenty-one months we find Mr. Judson and Dr. Price prisoners of the Burmans; for seven months in the Ava death-prison, a part of the time crowded with more than a hundred others — English, Portuguese, and Burmans, political enemies of the king, state officers in disgrace, thieves, cut-throats, deserters, English soldiers, innocent victims, villains of every dye — into a single unventilated room, under the care of a jailer called by the Burmans 'the tiger-cat,' and bearing the brand of *loothat* (murderer) upon his breast, to whose mind human torture furnished the most enjoyable of pastimes; then driven six miles in shackles over burning sands, where every step left blood-tracks; then for seven months at Oung-pen-la, at first in a roofless shanty, whose condition testified to the truth of the report, that they were sent there to be burned as a sacrifice.

"Once at nightfall, while they were in the death-prison, there spread among the prisoners a rumor, that, at three in the morning, they were all to be executed. The hour drew near. Mr. Judson prayed audibly for them all; then each prayed silently. Still there was no stir. The hour passed. It *must* have passed, they felt, though they had no means of knowing the time. Soon their comic jailer opened the door, and showed them what they already suspected, — it was morning. They spoke to him of the rumor.

"'Oh, no! I could not spare my dear children yet, just after having taken so much care to provide them with fitting ornaments;' and, as he spoke, he kicked the bamboo pole to which they were fastened, till the five pair of fetters of each clanked together, grinding the cringing flesh between them.

"Nearly every day for the first five months, Mrs. Judson might be seen, dressed in saffron vest and rich silken skirt (for she had adopted the Burman dress to please the natives), walking the two miles from her house to the prison, bearing food or clothing for the prisoners. Nearly every day she visited the palace, and talked with members of the royal family, hoping through them to influence the king. But day after day brought news of English success; and, while that continued, whoever spoke a kind word for a prisoner to his Majesty must do it at the peril of his life. Sometimes she was forbidden to see her husband: then they corresponded by means of tiles, on which the writing was invisible when wet, but became legible again after drying; or by slips of paper inserted in the long nose of the pot in which she sent his tea. Sometimes she could see him only in the evening; then she walked the long two miles back to her house alone, after dark.

"At one time she heard that her house was

to be searched. She decided to secrete her silver and various other little articles, — a desperate expedient; for their discovery might mean death. But to be without these things must mean starvation: so she carried out her plan, though with much trembling. The still more precious manuscript of the Burman New Testament, completed just before they left Rangoon, she had already sewed up in a pillow so hard that even a Burman could not covet it, and committed it to Mr. Judson's keeping.

"The officers saw her agitation, and apologized for the work they were about to do.

"'Where are your silver, gold, and jewels?' asked the royal treasurer.

"'I have no gold or jewels,' Mrs. Judson answered: 'but here is the key of the trunk which contains the silver; do with it as you please.'

"The trunk was produced, and the silver weighed.

"'This money,' said Mrs. Judson, 'was collected in America from the disciples of Christ, and sent here for the purpose of building a kyoung, and for our support while teaching the religion of Christ. Is it suitable that you should take it?'

"'We will state this circumstance to the king, and perhaps he will restore it,' said one of them. 'But is this all the silver you have?'

"She could not tell a lie. 'The house is in your possession; search for yourselves,' she answered.

"'Have you not deposited silver with some person of your acquaintance?'

"'My acquaintances are all in prison. With whom should I deposit silver?'

"Trunks and drawers were examined, and various articles taken from them; but the things Mrs. Judson had secreted were not discovered. These served as a source of supply for the constant demands of hunger, pity, and Burman officials, during the long months that followed. Her clothing she saved by representing that it would be a disgrace to present articles partly worn before the king.

"After five months Mrs. Judson was allowed to build a little bamboo room within the prison enclosure, and sometimes to spend two or three hours there with her husband. Then for a time she ceased to come entirely; and, when next the chained prisoner crawled forward to meet her, he found with her a little wailing, blue-eyed babe, born twenty days before.

"Mrs. Judson reached Oung-pen-la a few hours after the arrival of the prisoners, having followed with her babe on a Burmese cart, — a vehicle which would be counted among instruments of torture, if it were not a common mode of conveyance.

"The next morning, Moung Ing, walking past the prison, saw on the ground a hard roll of cotton, picked it up, and carried it home as a relic of the missionaries. It was the inside of Dr. Judson's pillow, which his keepers had restored to him in exchange for a better one after its first capture, and had robbed of its covering, and thrown away when he was driven from the prison the day before. In it, months later, was found the Burmese New Testament, unharmed.

"Before this, Bandula had been called back to Burmah, had been placed in charge of the main army, had fought, been defeated, and finally died. The Pakanwoon, who had been disgraced and imprisoned, offered to take his place, and conquer the English. His offer was accepted; and one of his first orders was for the removal and death of the prisoners; but, before it could be fully obeyed, he was himself arrested for treason, and, as a punishment, trodden to death by elephants.

"Repeated English victories at last led the Burman king to employ the missionaries in negotiating terms of peace. When finally the English terms were accepted, we find Mr. and Mrs. Judson, still weak from fever, sailing down the Irrawadi to the English camp.

"The English officers received them with the greatest honor. Every possible attention was shown Mrs. Judson, much to the surprise and alarm of the Burmans. Dr. Judson tells of one time particularly, when a grand dinner was given in the British camp, at which the Burman commissioners were guests. Mrs. Judson came in, leaning upon Gen. Campbell's arm. The Burman officers turned pale, with chagrin and fear.

"'Those seem to be old acquaintances of yours,' remarked the general; 'and, from their appearance, I judge you must have used them very badly. Who is yonder owner of the pointed beard?'

"Then Mrs. Judson told how—when she had walked miles to his house to ask a favor, which he roughly refused her, and was obliged to walk back again under a burning sun—he took from her her only umbrella, a silk one, and made sport of her request for its return, or at least a paper one in exchange.

"The Burman officer knew not a word of English; but conscience and memory were active interpreters. In vain Mrs. Judson told him softly in Burman that he had nothing to fear. The best efforts of the conquerors to put him and his companions at their ease utterly failed for that day. Mr. Judson said afterwards, 'I never thought I was over and above vindictive; but really it was one of the richest scenes I ever saw.'"

"It seems to me," remarked Walter, "that if the members of the council that refused admittance to Marshman and Ward in 1799, and expelled Judson and Newell in 1812, could have been there, it would have been rather a rich scene to them too."

"They would hardly have enjoyed seeing the missionaries made the especial favorites of the East India Company's officers, more than the Burmans did. But times had changed. Dr. Judson had done very much for both Burmah and England in those last weeks of the war, and his services were appreciated. Both governments wished to avail themselves of them for the future. The offer of the Burmans he declined; but he consented to accompany Dr. Crawford in an expedition to Ava, hoping thereby to gain religious toleration in Burmah.

"He was gone nearly seven months; and, when he returned, she whose almost superhuman labors had saved his life through the years of his imprisonment was at rest beneath the hopia-tree in Amherst. In a few weeks his babe was buried by her side."

"May I inquire what became of the eighteen converted at Rangoon?" said Clarence. "It seems the mission there was not continued."

"No; for Rangoon had been given back to Burmah, and there was no assurance of toleration there. As every field could not be cultivated, it seemed best to choose the most hopeful.

"Of the eighteen baptized, Mah Myatlah and Moung Thahlah had died before the war. Moung Shwa-gnong had died of cholera just after its close, and before he could join the missionaries. Of his record during those two years they learned nothing; but seven years later, as the Rangoon assistants passed up the river, they found at his home ten interesting inquirers, who had gained their knowledge of Christianity wholly from Moung Shwa-gnong, who, they said, 'preached and exhorted a great deal, and at one time spent a whole day and night talking on the subject with his neighbors.' Moung Shwa-ba had remained at the Rangoon mission-house through the war, and with Moung Ing, Mah Menla, and Mah Doke, joined the missionaries at Amherst. Three others would have been glad to do the same, but were prevented by the Burman Government from leaving Rangoon. The rest had died during the war, or been scattered into various parts of the country."

"Where was Dr. Price?" asked Walter.

"At Ava. He accepted an offer from the Burman king, and entered his service as a physician: there for a year he practised medicine, and lectured on astronomy, bending his knowledge of both always to the use of religion; and then, early in 1828, when he seemed most useful, died of pulmonary consumption."

"And the other missionaries?" asked Kate.

"Mr. and Mrs. Wade reached Amherst in November, 1826, a month after Mrs. Judson's death. Mr. and Mrs. Boardman, who had reached Calcutta in December, 1825, and remained there during the last part of the war, followed, but soon left for Maulmain.

"Before long it was decided that Maulmain, and not Amherst, should be the seat of government. The population of Amherst immediately declined, while Maulmain, two years before a wild jungle, had more than sixteen thousand inhabitants. Here, in the last months of 1827, Dr. Judson and the Wades, with some of the Rangoon converts, joined Mr. and Mrs. Boardman."

CHAPTER VII.

THE WILD MEN.

"MY story to-night begins with what has been called 'the romance of missions,'" said Mrs. Bancroft, "and I must introduce you to a new branch of our Eastern cousins; but you will hardly see either romance or cousins in them at first.

"Among the crowds that flocked past Dr. Judson's zayat at Rangoon, and, later, his wayside shed at Maulmain, might sometimes be seen a class of men lighter in color than the Burmans, and unlike them in feature and dress. They talked Burman with the Burmese, but among themselves spoke a strange language, that neither Burmans nor missionaries could understand. They came into the towns on business, talked on little except business, and left usually before nightfall. They looked with indifferent eyes upon gilded pagodas, stone Gaudamas, and yellow-robed priests and gods. Priests and Burmans looked with equal indifference upon them.

"'Who are they?' Dr. Judson asked the Burman disciples.

"'Only wild jungle people,' was the answer, as if wild jungle people were hardly people at all.

"If you had followed these men out of the town, you would have seen them going away to the mountains and plains, entering little villages, or clusters of long bamboo houses, built high from the ground for fear of wild beasts, and with all manner of filth and vermin beneath them, climbing each to his own apartment; and here at night you may find them, dirty, often drunken, sometimes fighting, yet generally truthful and honest. They scratch the surface of the ground, and raise grain enough for their own eating, perhaps a little more, to pay for taxes, or exchange for tools; if not, they borrow of the Burmans, and become their debtors, or, what in Burmah is about the same thing, their slaves.

"Their houses have no niches or shrines for

miniature Buddhas; but the 'spirits' that haunt all heathen and some Christian lands flock here in crowds. They have no priests; but there are clairvoyants or prophets among them, who are held in highest reverence, because they can see the (to all others invisible) spirits. True monarchs of the land are these spirits. If sickness comes, the spirit whose seat is in the back of the neck has left, and must be made to return, or the sufferer will become the victim of seven other spirits always waiting to devour, and die. If the paddy does not prosper, the spirits are to blame. Tigers, lions, alligators, are incarnate spirits. If cholera prevails, chickens, or perhaps a hog, must be sacrificed to the spirits. If a rooster crows in time of pestilence, his head comes off, lest he guide the malignant spirits to the house.

"That the spirits they worship, or the mediums through whom they consult them, are good, they do not pretend; nor will they deny that they may be closely connected with Satan. But they have lost the knowledge of God, and they evidently have not lost the knowledge of the Devil: so, like St. Christopher in the legend, they serve the stronger."

"But who are these people? and where did they come from?" asked Charlie.

"They are the Karens. Ask them their history, and they will tell you, that, long ago, their ancestors were expelled from the north country; that, led by an inspired guide, they crossed the river of sand; that then they had books of skin, containing the knowledge of God, but they lost them; that their fathers had taught them that some time the white foreigners would come and bring back again the book of God. What a 'book of skin' is they have not the slightest idea. Their only books now are those the missionaries have given them; but they will sing you songs like these, which their fathers have sung to them for generations back:—

"'God is eternal; his life is long.
God is immortal; his life is long.
One kalpa, he dies not;
Two kalpas, he dies not.
He is perfect in meritorious attributes;
Kalpas on kalpas he dies not.'

"Or,

"'In ancient times God created the world:
All things were minutely ordered by him.

He appointed the fruit of trial;
He gave minute orders.
Satan deceived two persons:
He caused them to eat the fruit of the tree of trial.
When they ate the fruit of trial
They became subject to sickness, old age, and death.'

"Or perhaps you will hear words like these:—

"'God is not far off. He is among us. He has only separated himself from us by a single thickness of white cloth. Children, it is because men are not upright that they do not see God.'"

"Very much like the Bible," suggested Clarence.

"Yes; and they have traditions of the creation, the fall, the dispersion, so *very* much like the Bible, that no one can doubt that some time, somewhere, the two currents of story must have come from the same fountain."

"But where did they separate?" asked Katie. "at the beginning, or in the days of the Jews, or since Christ's time?"

"That is one of God's secrets, and probably will always be so. All we know is, that, for generations, the Karens have been a nation in the midst of idols, hating idolatry, surrounded and conquered by Buddhists, yet believing in an eternal God.

"Before the war, the Karens were at the mercy of the Burmans. If a Burman wanted money or rice or work, or any thing else that a Karen had, he usually got it; and for this reason, among others, the Karens chose their homes in mountains and glens away from the city. In one of these out-of-the-way nooks, about the time that young Carey began to plead the cause of the heathen in England, there was born a Karen boy, Moung Thah-byu. He made a world of trouble for his parents and everybody that knew him till he was fifteen, when he left home to become a robber and murderer. How many he had killed, or helped others kill, he could not tell, when, at the close of the war, he entered Mr. Hough's service at Rangoon; but it was certainly not less than thirty.

"After a while, Moung Shwaba paid a debt for him, and so gained a right to his services. He had only ordinary talent, a diabolical temper, and no disposition to learn. Moung Shwaba gave him up in despair, and was about sending him away, when Dr. Judson paid the debt-money, and took the half-savage into the mission family.

"Slowly this man waked up to the horror of

his murderous life, became deeply penitent, and asked admission to the little Burman church. It was refused. The disciples saw that still his temper often gained the victory over him, and could not see, as Dr. Judson could, how earnestly he struggled with it. But, in a few months more, the change became plain to all; and he was received by a unanimous vote.

"The missionaries had already seen, that, with thousands of miles of unbroken heathenism around them, they could not afford to concentrate all their force at Maulmain. In the spring of 1828 Mr. Boardman went to Tavoy. Moung, now Ko ·Thah-byu, — for he was no longer strictly a young man, — went with him, and was baptized there.

"And now, through jungles, over mountains, across streams, wading often in water up to the armpits, braving the fiercest opposition of the elements and of human hearts, Ko Thah-byu went, preaching among the Karen villages. Some laughed; some said, 'We will hear you when the busy season is over;' but some believed; and then from lip to lip, and town to town, through Tavoy, Mergui, and Tenasserim, went the message, 'The white foreigners have come, and brought the book of God.'

"Ko Thah-byu's first visit was to a village whose men were busy planting on the hillside. One who had remained behind brought the message to the others, 'A man has come who wants to tell his genealogy to us.' The villagers came together; and Ko Thah-byu preached Christ. One, the brother of the chief of the village, believed at once. In time he aided in leading nearly his whole village to Christ.

"Three times he went out, spending days or weeks alone in the wilderness. Then Mr. Boardman went with him. It was not easy work to travel through almost impassable ravines, among tiger-haunted forests, up rugged mountains, under a burning sun; lying at night, it might be, on the ground, in a drenching rain; weary, sometimes half famished. I hardly think any physician would recommend scenes like these to a young man already strongly inclined to consumption. But when the villagers brought out their offerings of fowls and plantains, and he heard the words, 'Ah! you have come at last; we have been longing to see you,' he felt well paid for all.

"Numbers of the Karens applied for baptism. Thirty-two were at different times accepted and baptized. Others Mr. Boardman promised to see again, and examine; but, in the midst of the work, his strength failed.

"Mr. Mason reached Tavoy in January, 1831; and, accompanied by him and Mrs. Boardman, Mr. Boardman was carried on a cot into the jungle to fulfil his promise.

"'The cause of God is of more importance than my health,' he said, when his wife saw how fast he was failing, and urged his returning before the baptism. 'Ministers often wish to die in the pulpit; but to die in the pulpit would be nothing to dying here in the midst of the Lord's work.'

"So, a little before sunset, he lay on his cot by the water-side, and watched the entrance into the visible church of thirty-four previously examined by himself, and now baptized by Mr. Mason. Two days later, while on his way home, he entered the church triumphant in heaven.

"And now for a year, while the Masons were learning the language, upon Mrs. Boardman and Ko Thah-byu rested the care of the Karen mission. Mrs. Boardman received visits, and directed inquirers, at the town: Ko Thah-byu made visits, and awakened inquirers, in the jungle.

"Mr. Wade had reduced the Karen language

OUR GOLD-MINE. 131

THE PLACE WHERE BOARDMAN WITNESSED THE BAPTISM OF 34 KARENS A FEW HOURS BEFORE HIS DEATH. IN THE YAVOY DISTRICT.

to writing; and early in 1830 Mr. Bennett, a missionary printer, arrived with his wife. With him came a printing-press. Nothing could have delighted the Karens more than the idea of again having books in their own language. Everywhere Ko Thah-byu went he scattered tracts, and parts of the Bible; and, far into the regions unvisited, the tracts seemed to scatter themselves. The young Karens were eager to learn. Ko Thah-byu, too, learned to read; but what was easy for them was hard for him, and soon many of the young disciples were in advance of him in learning. He was called to be a pioneer, and he saw it. Leaving Tavoy, he preached to the Karens about Maulmain, and, later, around Rangoon. From here Mr. Bennett writes in 1833, —

"'Ko Thah-byu complains that the Karens throng his house so that it is breaking down. Crowds have all day long been coming and going; and he has been busy preaching from morning till night. They are very urgent from Bassein and Mergui on the south and west, from Maubee and vicinity on the north, that Ko Thah-byu or some Karen teacher should come and teach them to read, and preach to them the gospel. They offer of their own accord to build zayats and schoolhouses.'"

"If only a hundred missionaries could have gone out among them then!" said Kate.

"If only a hundred could go out now!" said Mrs. Bancroft.

"Where was Dr. Judson?" asked Charlie.

"Doing a work that no other man could do, — translating the Bible into Burman; preaching meanwhile, as he had opportunity, from a little shed projected into one of the dirtiest, noisiest streets in Maulmain.

"About this time, in a note signed simply 'A Missionary,' he gave to the Board six thousand dollars, his entire patrimony."

"Too much of a sacrifice, I think," said Charles.

"Not more than God required of him," said Katie.

"And of us?" asked Walter.

"I doubt if it was any sacrifice at all," said Mrs. Bancroft. "Where God's cause is wholly our cause, there is no such thing as sacrificing for it.

"In 1830 Dr. Judson went to Rangoon. Here for months Ko Thaha had struggled to keep together the little Burman church. In January, 1829, he was ordained their pastor.

Not long after, Moung Ing was associated with him. In this region the Burmans were not, as at Maulmain and Tavoy, held under the paw of the British lion; and it was a dangerous thing to inquire: still there were inquirers. 'I asked Pastor Thaha to go with me,' Dr. Judson writes when about starting up the Irrawadi for Prome: 'but he thinks it quite impossible, on account of having so many irons in the fire, — that is, hopeful inquirers that he must stay to bring forward and baptize; and he is as solicitous and busy as a hen pressing about her chickens. It is quite refreshing to hear him talk on the subject, and to see what a nice, careful old shepherd he makes.'

"After returning to Maulmain, Dr. Judson made three long tours into the jungle, encouraging the Karen disciples, and preaching, sometimes to an assembly of earnest listeners, sometimes in a concert of crying children, barking dogs, and railing sceptics, to the Karen heathen; and almost everywhere there was some fruit.

"Then for two years he shut himself up, so far as he could, to his translation; and at the end of that time, on the last day of January,

1834, he was able to write, 'Thanks be to God, I can *now* say I have attained. I have knelt down before him with the last leaf in my hand, and implored his forgiveness for all the sins that have polluted my labors in this department, and his aid in future efforts to remove the errors and imperfections which necessarily cleave to the work. I have commended it to his mercy and grace. I have dedicated it to his glory. May he make his own inspired Word, now complete in the Burman tongue, the grand instrument of filling all Burmah with songs of praise to our great God and Saviour Jesus Christ. Amen.'"

"But you mustn't think we were not doing any thing in America all this time," interrupted grandpa. "We sent out Mr. Jones and his wife, and the Kincaids, and the Cutters, and Browns, and Miss Harrington in 1830, and the Hancocks in 1831, and in 1832 Mr. Simons and the Webbs, and Vintons, and Howards, and Comstocks, and Osgoods, and Miss Cummings. You see, the Karens were Christianizing us quite as fast as we were Christianizing them."

Katie was often the last to leave the room. Walter had never before been the last but one;

JUDSON WITH THE LAST LEAF OF THE BURMAN BIBLE.

but this time he lingered till all the rest had gone. Then he turned abruptly to Katie: —

"It's too mean," he said, "that I should be here making work, when there is so much work to be done, and men are giving their lives to do it. I sometimes feel like killing myself, so there'll be one less sinner to convert."

"Walter, that is dreadful."

"I know it; but I can't help it."

"But are you sure you will not 'make work' for anybody even then?"

"I don't know any thing at all about it."

"Neither do I; but I do know that God expects something more of us than merely not to make work. He expects us to be workers."

"That is easier said than done."

"I know it; but *we* have to say it, and the doing of it belongs to God: so I sometimes think the saying it is the hardest part, after all."

"You haven't been much of a worker always, Kate."

"I know it: I am sorry."

Ten minutes of silence, and the two parted, understanding each other better than they ever had before.

CHAPTER VIII.

JUNGLE AND CITY.

"PLEASE read Minnie's letter."

Minnie stood by Walter's chair with a folded paper in her hand. All bits of paper were "letters" to her.

Walter looked up from the newspaper which he was *not* reading, unfolded the letter, glanced at it, and gave it back.

"Ida, read Minnie's letter."

Ida took the paper from Minnie's hand, and opened it, not expecting to find writing in it. But she did find it, and in Katie's hand; and this is what she read: —

"A missionary must be, —

"1. Patient, not easily discouraged or vexed. — *Carey.*

"2. Enthusiastic, but with an enthusiasm that will hold out when it has nothing external to support it. — *Judson.*

"3. Quick to see opportunities of usefulness, and ready to seize them, without asking questions or making excuses. — *Boardman.*

"4. Prudent and daring; braving every thing that need be braved for Christ's sake, and nothing that need not be. —*Mrs. Judson.*

"5. Unselfish, wholly consecrated to the cause. All the really successful missionaries are examples.

"6. Ready in acquiring languages. — *Carey, Wade.*

"7. Skilful in domestic matters, versatile, quick to devise expedients. — *Mrs. Judson.*

"8. Able to maintain a Christian life without the help of Christian society.

"All this I am not. Some part of it, by God's grace, I may yet become. Still I do not believe God has called me to the work of a foreign missionary; but he does call all who love him to the missionary work somewhere. *My work, I think, is here.*"

After Ida had read the paper through, it occurred to her that she had really no right to read it at all. She replaced it upon Katie's desk.

"Well, Ida?" said Walter.

"Well."

"When are you going to start?"

"Start? Where?"

"For India. I believe Minnie's letter is a pretty fair description of your character, as you've usually proclaimed it to us. I should think you would see a very clear call."

"Nonsense!"

When Katie returned to the room, a glance at the open paper on her desk, and an exchange of glances with Ida, told her what had happened.

"How much Katie is changed!" thought Ida. "She would have been terribly angry if I had read any such thing of hers, once."

"How much Ida is changed!" thought Katie. "She would have given me a long congratulo-triumphant lecture, if she had discovered anything of that sort, once."

Both thoughts occurred to Walter, and he whistled a commentary upon them; but, unfortunately, there has never been written a dictionary for the interpretation of whistling.

Walter's remark was not entirely nonsense: if it had been, it would not have intruded itself upon Ida's mind a dozen times in the course of the day, haunting her even after Mrs. Bancroft had begun her story in the evening.

"If you had traversed the jungles about Tavoy in the dry season of 1831, you might very possibly have met, emerging from some ruinous zayat, or coming up dripping from the fording of a stream, or perhaps, weary with travel over untrodden roads and bridgeless rivers, stopping with her company of Karen followers to dine in some wayside shed, a lady as refined and delicate as any who to-day are reclining on American sofas, consecrating their lives to headaches and dyspepsia. It was Mrs. Boardman. In this way she kept up her acquaintance with the Karens of the wilderness. Frequently she led the worship in their assemblies.

"During the rainy season she was not less busy in the city, instructing the women, directing the assistants, and superintending schools. A few months later, you might have found Mr. Mason in the same city, preaching Christ to the priests and worshippers of its thousand pagodas, and, after the rains, crossing and recrossing the same jungles. Let us follow, and see him at his work.

"Here, under a shed, bowing with clasped hands before a gilded Gaudama, and praying, 'O Lord, preserve us!' are some Burmans.

"'What is the use of talking to that image, whose ears cannot hear?' he asks.

"'We pray, sir, to Gaudama, who has gone to Nigban,' is the answer.

"'Has he a body there?'

"'No.'

"'Has he a mind?'

"'No.'

"'And what can a person know without mind or body?'

"A hearty laugh, the usual Burman covering for defeat, is the only reply.

"Here are some women, cooking under the trees.

"'Where do you expect to go after death?' he asks one of them.

"'Oh! I shall be put into the ground yonder.'

"'Where will your soul go?'

"'I am a woman, and know nothing about that.'

"He reaches Thabu village: there are three houses of Christians here, and eight or nine apply for baptism.

"'What sins have you committed?' he asks of one.

"'I have worshipped the earth, fire, demons, pagodas, images, and have sinned with every member of my body.'

"'That's enough,' interrupts Ko Thah-byu.

"The examination goes on. This woman

and five others are accepted and baptized : two or three are rejected. The Lord's Supper is celebrated, a marriage solemnized; and the mis-

sionary passes on to That Creek, a village mainly Christian. An old woman totters out to meet him. She is one of those whom he baptized by the bedside of the dying Boardman.

"'I think of God continually,' she says, 'and of dwelling in his presence forever.'

"'Do you have no quarrelling or scolding among you now?' he asks.

"'No.'

"'No, sir,' answers the headman, a notorious drunkard. 'There is no trouble with those who have been baptized.'

"And now he comes to Mata, the City of Love. Here are two hundred Christians gathered into a village of their own. They hold meetings, and every convert is ready to speak or pray. They send out missionary companies into the jungle, and give their money to print tracts. The women spin and weave, and wash the garments which were never washed before. The men have goats and cattle, ploughs and oil-mills. The children are trained to be Christians; those whose parents were drunkards growing up without even knowing the sight of liquor. The ground under their houses is swept: the vermin that once burrowed there, and the Nats that filled the spiritual atmosphere, have fled together. Instead of sacrifices to demons, from almost every house ascend prayer and praise to God. Daily at sunrise the people meet at the zayat for worship. 'The town of Mata, amid the solitudes of the great mountains of Tavoy,' writes Dr. Malcom, 'exhibits facts, which, if they were all the effects our mission could boast, are sufficient to assure the most incredulous of the blessedness of our enterprise. The only punishment I would inflict on the enemies of missions would be a pilgrimage to these villages.'

"In 1834 Mrs. Boardman left Tavoy for Maulmain, the wife of Dr. Judson. In the same year, Miss Cummings, who, before she knew the language, had gone to Chummerah alone with the Burman teachers, and there, with the native assistants, had carried on the station for two years, left it, sick with the jungle-fever, to find a grave in Maulmain.

"In the first days of 1835 the Masons welcomed the Wades back to share their labors; and here, after a dozen years of monotonous variety, we find them still. Let us glance at them a few times during those twelve years.

"It is evening. They have travelled all day through jungles which no horse could penetrate, sometimes climbing steep cliffs, sometimes walking on the very edge of precipices two or three hundred feet high, till, thoroughly tired, they reach the Christian village of Quagthah. The disciples flock out, and offer their houses. But the night is damp, the houses crowded; and the missionaries will not allow them to endanger their women and little ones. They spread comforters, and lie upon the ground; but the Christian Karens come out and lie down around them, that, 'should the tigers come in the night, they may take them, and not the missionaries.'

"They reach Mata; and Mrs. Wade remains there, while the men go on a long journey into the jungle. Saturday comes, and the disciples cluster around her.

"'Will not the mamma preach to us tomorrow?'

"'God has not appointed women to preach,' she answers; 'but we will sit down together as brothers and sisters, and I will read and explain some of the words of our Saviour.'

"She 'read and explained' to a congregation of one hundred and fifty. Through the week she ministered to a score of sick and dying, singing as she went, —

> 'Oh that the Lord would count me meet
> To wash his dear disciples' feet!'

"It was well she appreciated the privilege: for the feet of Christian Karens even are not always clean; and, if they were, it was not pleasant, in visiting some sick disciple, to find his friends in the room broiling a snake, or cooking a dish of black ants for dinner.

"The next Sunday there were one hundred and sixty at worship. Many were inquirers, some recent converts; and when, at the end of six weeks, Mr. Wade again joined her, twenty-five were ready for baptism.

"Later, we find Mr. Wade and Mr. Mason with their followers at Tamler. Several of the people had died of dysentery; and the rest, for miles around, were panic-stricken, and determined to run away. In one house lay a man and child sick with the disease, a wife with a little babe, and a child dead, and none to bury it.

"'Can you not go and bury it?' Mr. Mason asked the Christian Karens.

"They hesitated. 'We are afraid. The disease is certainly infectious,' they answered.

"'Then I will go,' said Mr. Mason.

"Their courage quickened by this, the disciples went with him; and together, after fighting their way through the bushes in the dark for two or three miles over ground where a man had been devoured by a tiger in broad daylight not long before, they reached the place, dug a grave, and gave the child Christian burial. Deeply moved by such strange kindness, the parents promised to become Christians. The next year Mr. Mason found, to his surprise, that the promise had been kept.

"Time brought new work and new workers. San Quala, the second Karen convert, led to Christ by Ko Thah-byu's first sermon, is now an active evangelist, accompanying Mr. Mason on his long tours, and giving sermons that would do honor to many an American preacher; while by carefully watching the modes of labor, the examination of candidates, and the discipline of transgressors, he is fitting himself for a far greater work hereafter. Mata has nearly doubled in size; and in scores of places the jungle is lighted by the tiny tapers of Christian churches. Every time the missionaries go out among the churches, there are candidates for discipline as well as for baptism. Here are some that have fallen into intemperance; others that have worshipped the Nats; another that has 'used cursing language to her dog;' another who said to her child, 'May the tigers eat you!' Twenty have been absent from sabbath worship; some only for one sabbath, however. One has been guilty of foolish talking; three, of calumny. So read the records of the Mata church, as kept by the Karen clerk, and reported to the missionaries. One cannot help thinking how some American church-records would read, if kept as carefully.

"All these cases the missionary must attend to. Then sickness visits the flock; and his wife is nurse, physician, every thing. With her own hands she washes the leprous sores, or prepares cooling draughts for the husband, while his wife stands speechless and trembling. With her own hands she takes the fevered child from its helpless mother, and nurses it alone; for the Karens know nothing of medicine or nursing, except through charms. The fever heightens; and then comes the agonizing question, —

"'*May* I not make *one* offering to the Nats?'

"'No.' It is a hard word even for the teacher to speak, with those pitiful eyes looking into her own, pleading for leave to do the one only thing the mother knows how to do to save her child.

"The hours pass by,—hours in which the missionary struggles hand to hand with death, and the mother with all the powers of temptation.' The child grows worse.

"'Only *once*! Would it be wrong?' pleads the mother.

"'The Nats cannot help you, but God can,' answers the missionary.

"The mother *cannot* disbelieve in the Nats. Has she not seen them, heard them, made offerings to them, and been helped by them? Have not her neighbors talked with them? Are they not even now tormenting her child? The Nats may be wicked: but surely there *are* Nats; and not to offer to them is to sacrifice her child. *Will* God require it? But the mother obeys. A few more busy, anxious hours, and morning shows the fever gone from the child, and, better still, the terror of the Nats gone from the mother's heart forever; for her God has shown himself stronger than they. But many another Karen mother, who has bravely stood all other tests, facing alone this terrible temptation, has fallen before it.

"While so much of the strength of the mission was diverted to the jungle, the great cities were not forgotten.

"While learning the language, Mr. Kincaid took charge of a little European church started among the soldiers at Maulmain, and ninety-five were added to its numbers. In 1833 he sailed up the Irrawadi to Ava. Almost everywhere he found some who were willing to listen."

"Was it thanks to Bibles or British powder?" asked Clarence.

"To the British powder, no doubt, that he could preach unmolested in all the three hundred villages between Rangoon and Ava; but it was not British powder that had scattered tracts and whispered fragments of the gospel message in advance of him in regions no missionary had ever trodden, or that kindled a longing for it in scores of hearts of those who heard now for the first time.

"Once, as he was busy giving tracts to the crowd that lined the shore, a young man came with the request, 'Will you please give me St. John's history of Christ and the Acts of the Apostles?'

"The books were given, with four tracts, and the young man disappeared; but at dark he came again.

"'There is a man besides me in the city who

believes in Jesus Christ, and he wants to see the teacher and get books; but he thinks the boat is away, and has sent me to search.'

"Following him, Mr. Kincaid found a venerable man, who, with only St. John and the Acts to teach him, had for two years been leading a Christian life. The young man had heard Dr. Judson preach in Prome, and received from him the books which he had read to his friend. Now both were open disciples. Mr. Kincaid spent with them an evening never to be forgotten.

"When settled in Ava, he found a congregation of seven or eight hundred frequently clustering about the zayat where he preached, while visitors crowded his veranda.

"One day he sent out Ko Shun and Ko San Lone to occupy a large zayat in another part of the city. Arrived there, they found Moung Kay, a popular young Buddhist preacher, discussing and explaining his sacred books to the people. They listened respectfully till he paused.

"'Have you heard that there is a God eternal, who is not, and never was, subject to any of the infirmities of men?' they asked him.

"'No.'

"'There is such a God, and his sacred Word is in Burmah.'

The Lord's Prayer in Burmese.

ဘိုဥ့်ရှိတော်မူသောအကျွန်ုပ်တို့အဖ။ ကိုယ်တော်၏
ုသော လေးမြတ်ခြင်း ရှိပါစေသော။ နိူင်ငံတော်တည်
၁။ အလိုတော်သည်ကောင်းကင်ဘိုဥ့်ပြည့်စုံသကဲ့သို့
ည့်စုံပါစေသော။ အသက်မွေးလောက်သောအစာ
ားနေ့ရက်အစည်အတိုင်းပေးသနားတော်မူပါ။ သူ
ျွန်ုပ်တို့ကို ပြစ်မှား သောအပြစ်များကို အကျွန်ုပ်တို့
သို့အကျွန်ုပ်တို့၏အပြစ်များကိုလွှတ်တော်မူပါ။ အ
ဆသို့ မလိုက်စေဘဲ မကောင်း သော အမှု အရာ နှင့်
ု့အကြောင်းကယ်မသနားတော်မူပါ။ "အာမင်။

---

o art in heaven, hallowed be thy name; thy king-
vill be done in earth, as it is in heaven. Give us
ly bread; and forgive us our debts, as we forgive
l lead us not into temptation, but deliver us from
s the kingdom, and the power, and the glory, for-

The Lord's Prayer in Karen.

၁မူခိၣ်ဧၢ။ ကစၢ်အမံၤနေၣ်မ်ပှၤပာ်စီဆှံကးအိတ
၃အမူနေၣ်မ်အတုၤကေၤတကော်။ဖဲကစၢ်အသးမ်အ
၁ခိၣ် အချၢအံၤ ဒ်လၢမူခိၣ် အသိး နေၣ်တကော်။ အ
ဒုလၢ်ပှၤလၢပဘုၣ်အိဘုၣ်အိပသးအံတကော်။ ပှၤ
ၤမၣ်ဘၣ်ပှၤဖိး ဒ်ပပျှၢ်ကွံာ်အတၢ် ဒဲးဘး သိး နေၣ်ပ
ၢ်ကွံာ်တကော်။ သုတဒုးလဲၤပှၤဆူတၢ်လေၤပစိအပှၤ
ၤမၢ်တၢ်အၢတၢ်သိ နေၣ်မၤပှၤမၤဖှဲးလၢ်အီၤဒီး ပှၤ

"They read to him the catechism and part of the 'View.'

"'Will you give me a book?'

"The book was given. He read incessantly till he had finished the New Testament and all the tracts. On the fifth day he threw away his beads, and forsook the pagodas. Soon he became a frequent visitor at the veranda.

"'How shall I know that I have a new heart?' he asked at one time.

"'When you love Christ, his word, and his people, when you love holiness, and hate idolatry and all sin, you may know that you have a new heart.'

"There was a long pause; and then the young preacher said, 'I think I have a new heart. I see every thing differently from what I formerly did. Every thing is so new, that I can hardly eat or sleep.'

"A few days later he asked to be baptized, but in the night.

"'Are you afraid to advocate the cause of Christ?'

"'No; but my family are afraid.'

"So the first to be baptized was a woman, Mah May Oo.

"'I know it is the true religion,' she said, 'because it takes away my pride, and makes me feel like a little child.'

"But, the next Lord's Day, Moung Kay followed; and in the course of time a church of twenty-one was gathered. Still every convert was snatched like a bone from between the tiger's jaws. The Burman officers coaxed, warned, and threatened violence. Mr. Kincaid was compelled to live out of the city limits, and to stop giving tracts against Buddhism; but as long as he was not absolutely forbidden by the king to preach, and give Testaments, he would not leave the capital.

"But a few months later, on returning from a perilous trip of three hundred and fifty miles to the foot of the Himalayas, he found a new king on the throne, all teaching of the Christian religion absolutely forbidden, and grave mutterings of war with England. He left his band of twenty-one disciples, and went to Rangoon, and soon after to Maulmain.

"Now let us look at Rangoon. I think Dr. Judson must have appreciated the place as a training-school for missionaries; for nearly every new one was for a longer or shorter time stationed there. It was the hardest of fields. 'To get a new convert,' Dr. Judson writes in 1831, 'is like pulling the eye-teeth out of a live tiger.' Yet, when Mr. Webb came in 1834, he baptized thirty-one Karens, and there were many more applicants.

"In 1835 there came a general persecution. Mr. and Mrs. Howard were the only missionaries there, and almost wholly ignorant of the language; when one morning Ko San-Lone, one of the native pastors, came in with the news that a petty officer had sent for him.

"'What shall I do?'

"'You had better go with him, and Moung Shway Thah shall go with you.'

"Soon Moung Shway Thah came back with the news that Ko San-Lone was confined for examination. In the afternoon Mr. Howard went himself to the Woongyee with an English interpreter.

"'Ah! this is the American teacher. What does he want?'

"'One of the rulers has confined one of my men, and I have come to see about it.'

"'What has he shut him up for?'

"'I do not know.'

"'I think he gives writings the ruler does not like,' said the Woongyee; and, turning to the interpreter, 'Tell him to let him go.'

"When the mob heard the message, they rushed in a mass to the Woongyee's house, and brought all manner of false charges against Ko San-Lone, until at last he was given over to their mercies. For weeks he lay in prison, loaded with torturing chains, often beaten, and threatened with death if he continued his refusal to worship Gaudama. Daily, as the native Christians walked the streets, they heard the question, 'When is that Christian going to be executed?'. But he remained firm and happy in his faith; and at last, by the payment of all he had and sixty rupees from the missionaries, he was released. 'Through all this,' Mr. Webb says, 'not a word escaped his lips which savored of irritation. Indeed, in looking over all I have ever seen of him or heard, I do not remember a single word or act which I could wish altered. He was at all times the humble, spiritual Christian. A few months after his release he died.'

"Through all the region the Christian Karens were fined, often to an amount far more than all they had. None dared come to the mission-house. Mr. Howard could not even employ a teacher. Yet persecution bore its fruit; and when, soon after, Messrs. Vinton, Abbott, and Howard went up the Irrawadi to Maubee, they baptized one hundred and seventy-three. Ko Thah-byu had been preaching there, and these were mainly the result of his labors. Later, Mr. Abbott baptized thirty-seven in the same neighborhood.

"'These public baptisms may bring on persecution,' he suggested.

"'If they persecute, let them persecute,' was the answer.

"At first the persecutions were slight, with long intervals of quiet. At one time, the missionaries who had left Rangoon were even invited back by the viceroy, that, seeing them at work, the people might feel sure there was no prospect of war. But the mild viceroy was soon deposed; a sterner took his place; and the Karen Christians were hunted as their fellow-citizens, the tigers, had never been. They were fined, imprisoned, beaten, killed. Many fled across the mountain to Arracan, where Mr. Abbott was now stationed; many perished on the way there. All communication with the foreigners was forbidden, so that a missionary to the Burmans might as well be in Boston as in Rangoon; and so, very reluctantly, the mission was given up to the native assistants.

"For several years, a great part of Dr. Judson's time was occupied by the revision of the Bible. His voice had failed now, so that his preaching could not often be distinctly heard. Thus Providence seemed to join in the call the Board had for some time been making upon him, to prepare a dictionary for the use of future missionaries; and he commenced the work.

"In 1845, as the only chance of saving Mrs. Judson's life, he left with her for America. She lived only to reach the Island of St Helena. There she was buried. In October, Dr. Judson, with his three children, arrived in Boston.

"It was thirty-three years since the first missionaries left America. Its old men were all dead, its middle-aged men old, its children middle-aged men. The children of 1845 knew Judson's name as they knew the names of Luther and Knox and Whitefield. To have a man step out from the pages of history into their streets and churches was a new experience. America was a still stranger sight to Judson.

Except the changes that he and his brethren and the war of 1825 had brought, the Burmah of 1845 was the Burmah of 1812. There had been a few revolutions, to be sure; but, in the East, revolutions belong to the ordinary course of events, and their absence would mark a far greater change than their presence. But the America he found was less like the America he left than the men now in its pulpits were like the infants then in its cradles. The nation had grown from boyhood to manhood in thirty-three years.

"As the ship came to land, Dr. Judson was considerably troubled lest he should not know where to look for lodgings; never dreaming that a hundred houses would be proud to claim him as their guest, and crowds everywhere be eager to hear the few low words that his voice had strength to utter. Why should they? He had only done very imperfectly his duty. Many of them had done more, he hoped. Was it a so much greater thing to do one's duty in Burmah than in America, that people must flock to see him for that?

"He spoke briefly a few times in public, — never of himself, rarely of his mission, but always of Christ. An audience that gathered to hear descriptions of Burman customs, or of thrilling adventures, was sure to be disappointed.

"An intimate friend mentioned this disappointment to him at one time.

"'Why, what did they want?' he inquired. 'I presented the most interesting subject in the world to the best of my ability.'

"'But they wanted something different, — a story.'

"'Well, I am sure I gave them a story the most thrilling that can be conceived of.'

"'But they had heard it before. They wanted something new from a man that had just come from the antipodes.'

"'Then I am glad they have it to say, that a man coming from the antipodes had nothing better to tell them than the wondrous story of Jesus' dying love.'

"Amid applause that would have more than satisfied most men, Dr. Judson was homesick for Burmah. The last days of November, 1846, found him again within sight of its shores. With him sailed Mrs. Emily C. Judson (whom he had married just before leaving America), Messrs. Harris and Beecher with their wives, and Miss Lillybridge.

"Nor was it enough to be on heathen soil. He hungered for the land of prisons and persecutions (Burmah Proper), and was not satisfied till he was settled in Rangoon, in the upper story of a brick den, almost windowless, gloomy as a prison, and already occupied by innumerable bats, which flared up through the night with a sound reminding him of Niagara. He was pastor of a church of twelve re-organized from the old Rangoon church, and preached to a congregation of twenty, who came on Sunday morning, one or two at a time, bringing parcels, or dishes of fruit, or wearing their clothes tucked up like coolies to avoid suspicion, and in the afternoon left as gradually."

"It takes a deal to satisfy some men," remarked Walter. "It is well all D.D.'s are not so ambitious."

"I confess, I am glad I am more easily contented," said Clarence.

"I doubt if he was fully contented until the 6th of June, when he had the privilege of leading down a young convert to the tank, where, twenty-eight years before, he insulted the stone Gaudama by the baptism of Moung Nau. This was the second baptism since he came to Rangoon.

"The next day the young man's father, an old disciple, was arrested, and brought to the governor's court. Dr. Judson was told of it, and for two hours sat expecting the worst.

"'What have you brought the man before me for?' asked the officer of the accusers.

"'To be examined on the charge of heresy, and of frequenting the house of Jesus Christ's teacher,' said the leader.

"'On what authority?'

"'Here is your written order.'

"'What? Who? I have given no order. It must be one of my petty clerks. It's all a mistake. Go about your business.'

"'I thought it strange,' rallied the prisoner, 'that you should summon me on the charge of heresy, since it is well known that I worship the true God.'

"'God!' exclaimed the officer, a little nettled. 'Worship any God you like.'

"'Or the Devil,' added a virago at his side. 'If you villagers pay your taxes, what more do we want?'

"Yet the officer *had* given the order. But probably, after his servants had been sent to execute it, he had shown it to the governor; and the old man, remembering a pledge he had made to Dr. Judson, quashed the proceeding.

"At any rate, the jaws of death were closed that time without taking in the disciple; but Dr. Judson's house was watched, and no one dared come near it on Sunday."

"Wasn't it a little strange," said Charlie as Mrs. Bancroft closed, "that, at the very time the Karens were counting converts by the hundreds in spite of persecution, Maulmain, with its dozen missionaries, could only boast one hundred and fifty converted Burmans?"

"Not very," replied Clarence. "Christianity does not seem adapted to the wants of scholarly races like the Hindoos and Burmans so well as to more barbarous people like the Karens. Its successes are always among tribes not capable of great intellectual development."

"The English and Americans, for example," remarked Walter gravely.

Mrs. Bancroft smiled. "The best answer I can give to Charlie's question," she said, "is an illustration Dr. Judson used in a sermon about this time. There is used in the East a kind of earth-oil, so vile in smell, that no dish once used for it can be fit for any thing else. The illustration ran about like this: There are two jars, one empty, the other full of earth-oil. A man goes to the owner of the empty jar, and asks if he may fill it with pure water. 'Oh, yes! I shall consider it a favor,' is the answer. So the Karens receive the gospel. Then he goes to the owner of the jar of earth-oil. First he must empty it. This the owner considers robbery. 'You are taking away my property,' he says: 'I will apply to the king and priests to uphold me in clinging to my property.' After long persuasion, the man consents to give up his oil. Then comes dipping out and washing and rubbing, the man all the while begging him not to take it *all* away. At last the water is poured in: but, after all, so much of the old oil clings to the dish, that the bystanders say, 'We do not perceive that the water is sweeter than the oil;' and perhaps, after a while, the man himself joins in, says the smell is as bad as before, and upsets the jar. So it is in religion. The Karens, who have little to give up, receive Christ gladly: the Burmans, who have much, are slow to part with it; and, when they do, the old religion too often makes its mark upon the new.

"In 1840 Mr. Abbott and Mr. Kincaid joined

the mission in Arracan. Here for five years the Comstocks had been laboring. Two years later Mr. and Mrs. Hall joined them, but died before their work began. Mr. and Mrs. Stilson came in 1839, and were now stationed at Ramree. Mr. Kincaid went to Akyab. Mr. Abbott located himself at Sandoway, that he might look after the Karens; but for some days no Karens were visible. As they seemed not likely to come to him, he went out to one of their villages. He talked: they would not listen. He asked to enter their houses: they refused. To save himself from the scorching sun, he entered one uninvited, but was not allowed a seat. These were the people for whom he was perilling his life. The prospect was gloomy as it could well be.

"Yet even then, across the mountains, and far into Burmah Proper, the news had flown, that the teacher was once more within reach; and soon, in companies of five, ten, and twenty, they were flocking to see him. Some came to hear the gospel, some to remain and study, some for baptism. Burmah had been shut to the missionaries; but no emperor's edict could shut out the Holy Spirit. Some of the books scattered by the Rangoon missionaries had crossed to the border of the empire, and were in the hands of Karen Christians. One had given a rupee for a New Testament, another a day's work for a tract. One of the Burmans baptized by Mr. Kincaid at Ava had been made a ruler in Bassein, and not only refused to imprison Christians, but himself kept the sabbath, and prayed to the eternal God.

"One of the disciples, Bleh Poh, soon after his conversion, had a child fall dangerously sick.

"'You are the cause; you have forsaken the religion of your fathers, and the child's demon is angry with you,' said his friends: and they begged him to 'eat the Devil;' in other words, to offer a sacrifice to him.

"'I trust in the everlasting God, and have renounced the worship of devils,' said Bleh Poh.

"The child died. Bleh Poh was brought before the court.

"'He has a foreigner's book, and has embraced the foreigners' religion,' was the chief charge against him.

"'What is in the book?' asked the judge.

"Bleh Poh answered by giving in his own words an abstract of the Bible, closing with a kind but earnest sermon on idolatry.

"'What you say is all very good,' said the officer; 'but, if I do not take notice of this case, it will come to the ears of the king, and I shall lose my life.'

"'Don't fear. Send *me* up to the king, and let me answer for myself, or suffer.'

"Commonly, Karens thus arrested were fined, beaten, or imprisoned; but Bleh Poh's sermon had made such an impression, that he was released without either.

"He returned to his family, only to meet insults and curses from them.

"'You have murdered your child. We will kill you.'

"'If you do not kill me, I shall die myself soon,' he answered meekly.

"Soon his wife and several others of his relations became converts, while the Burman officer from that time favored the Christians.

"'The Karen Christians are a quiet, peaceable race, and pay their taxes,' he said, when told by a higher officer to put three or four of them to death as an example: 'if they wish to worship *their* God, let them.'

"The chance to testify for Christ before Burman officers came often; and so fearless and gentle was Bleh Poh, that he always made his judges either friends or *harmless* enemies. He was one of the first baptized by Mr. Abbott at Sandoway. At home he was humble, faithful, prayerful, generous, the arbiter of disputes, the adviser in difficulties; abroad he was a most earnest, self-sacrificing preacher. He died in the last days of 1843, at the age of thirty.

"Ko Tha-byu came with Mr. Abbott to Sandoway. He had been the first to preach Christ to the Karens of Tavoy, of Maulmain, and of Rangoon, and now was ready to aid in opening the work in Arracan. But, at the beginning of his work, God took him. He died willingly and fearlessly a few months after his arrival. In reply to all questions as to the future, his answer was, 'Teacher, the Lord will preserve me.'

"In 1841 Bleh Poh's brother appeared, with eight others, as an applicant for baptism.

"'Can you bear persecution and death for Christ?' asked Mr. Abbott, 'or will you deny your Lord?'

"He hesitated: he *thought* he should not 'do as Peter did.'

"'Dare you testify before God and this congregation that you will endure unto death?'

"'I am afraid, teacher. I dare not.'

"Mr. Abbott repeated the question. A large congregation waited in breathless silence and anxious expectation.

"He bowed his face to the floor, and wept. They needed no such proof of his sincerity; yet, having asked the question, Mr. Abbott dared not let it pass unanswered. The assembly was still as the grave.

"At last he raised his head. Great tears rolled down his cheeks.

"'I think — teacher — I shall *not* — deny the Lord — if he gives me grace. I can say no more.'

"His request for baptism was joyfully granted.

"Others of Bleh Poh's relatives were dreadfully beaten, bound with fetters, and imprisoned.

"'Do you worship the eternal God?' asked an officer of one of them.

"'Yes.'

"'Well, you must worship no more.'

"'I shall worship, though you kill me.'

"'These Karen Christians are a very hard case,' said the officer.

"Of such the teachers had no fears; but all were not such. And now the clouds thickened;

the persecution became fierce. The times of baptism were times of deepest solemnity; for to many of them the rite shadowed forth more than *figurative* death and burial. Some apostatized: it could hardly be otherwise among so many thousands. Many were faithful to death. Hundreds fled across the mountains to Arracan, and, with Mr. Abbott's help, found there food and shelter and religious liberty. They had just laid out a new village, when with summer came cholera, and very many of them in the strange climate fell victims to it, or were driven back panic-stricken to the jungle, to die there.

"'My hands are full of labor, and my heart full of care, sometimes of *anguish*,' Mr. Abbott wrote in May, 1844, — 'nearly a thousand baptized converts, many of them suffering under the iron arm of a ruthless despotism; two hundred families of emigrants, who have fled from persecution, leaving *all* their worldly stores, and looking to me for food till they can reap a harvest; thirty native preachers to teach and guide and govern; two ordained pastors to watch and *tremble* over; elementary books to write and translate: add to this a sick family, and not a good night's rest for many months.'

"Around Akyab there were everywhere those hesitating between the two religions.

"From the Kemmees there came one day a mountain chief, Chetza, with some of his followers. Mr. Kincaid talked with him. He listened with the usual native indifference; but a few weeks later there came a letter, signed by him and thirteen minor chiefs, begging for a missionary, offering to build dwellings and schoolhouses at his own expense, giving the names of two hundred and seventy-three who would be scholars. When the missionaries visited him, and promised to try to grant his request, he was delighted.

"'Your decision gives me more joy than hundreds of gold and silver,' he said: 'they would soon be expended; but, if we have the knowledge of God, I shall die in peace.'"

"Who went?" asked Charlie.

"*Nobody.* The missionaries already there had their hands full, and there were no new ones. There are no words to express the feelings of those on the ground as they saw the tens of thousands that might so easily be reached, with Buddhism, Popery, and infidelity stretching out eager hands to grasp them, and among them all only three Christian preachers.

"'*Must* this promising harvest be *forever lost?*' wrote Mr. Stilson. '*Can* not and *will* not the many Baptist Christians in America spare the crumbs which fall from their tables for the famishing, dying thousands of Arracan?' wrote Mr. Comstock.

"In 1843 Mrs. Kincaid's health obliged Mr. Kincaid to leave with her for America. He took with him two of Mrs. Comstock's children.

"'This I do for my Saviour,' she said, as she looked upon them for the last time, and placed them in his hands.

"'Remember, brother, six men for Arracan,' was Mr. Comstock's parting message.

"Before it reached America, Mrs. Comstock was called to the work above; and a year later the death of Mr. Comstock left Mr. and Mrs. Stilson again alone in Arracan."

"Were the Board asleep? What were they thinking about, that they didn't send the men there?" asked Katie.

"In the first number of the 'Magazine' for 1846 there is an article, made up mainly of figures and statistics, over which I shed more tears than I ever gave to a novel. In it the committee of the Board stand, like Mr. Dustin in our New-England histories, when, with the Indians behind and his children before, he had to decide which of the eight little ones he could save, and which must be given up to the enemy. You remember, Edith."

"'Now from those dear ones make thy choice.'
   The group he wildly eyed;
When 'Father!' burst from every voice,
   And 'Child!' his heart replied.

There's one that now can share his toil,
   And one he meant for fame,
And one that wears her mother's smile,
   And one that bears her name.

And one will prattle on his knee,
   Or slumber on his breast;
And one whose joys of infancy
   Are still by smiles expressed."

Edith repeated the lines slowly: she had learned them to recite at school.

"So," said Mrs. Bancroft, "the committee compared the missions, counting the cost, the results, the prospects, of each, to decide which should be abandoned. This one was abundant in conversions, that in inquirers; another was less fruitful. But could they, in the face of the prayers of those who had died for it, abandon it? Besides, it had been established less years than passed in Burmah before the first conversion; and the cost of abandoning the Burman and Karen missions they dared not compute. To another their faith had been pledged; others were the only hope of Christianity in wide fields. But, while they could not choose between the hungry souls crying for help from across the water, close behind them pressed the enemy, — *a growing debt.* The expenditures of the society had exceeded its receipts by forty thousand dollars."

"And American church-members called themselves Christians, and allowed that?" said Katie, her cheeks flushing with indignation.

"What would you have given if you had been there?" asked Walter.

"Every thing. Thousands, if I had had it. How could any Christian help it?"

Walter smiled.

"What do you mean?"

"From what I hear, I think the Board is in about the same fix to-day; and I suppose there are Khyens and Arracanese still living. I believe I'll write to Boston to know whether there isn't some vacancy in the treasury that *ten* dollars would just fill."

"You ought to be ashamed of yourself, Walter!" exclaimed Charlie. "Katie's been saving up that ten dollars for a year to buy a pair of chromos for her room, and you know it."

"Do the heathen have chromos in their rooms, mother?" asked Edith.

"Thank you, Walter," Kate whispered as she passed him and went up stairs.

CHAPTER IX.

SHADOW AND SUNLIGHT.

WHEN Katie went up stairs, and the bare walls of her room faced her, and the Karens that had seemed so near an hour before glided back to their homes in Burman jungles, it was not so easy to give up the chromos, and send the carefully saved ten dollars to the heathen, as she thought it when she thanked Walter for the suggestion. Still she was glad she *had* thanked him, and so committed herself.

On Sunday morning she opened her desk to take the money. She knew just where to lay her hand on it. It was in an old purse,—just ten dollars, and no more; and yet, opening the porte-monnaie, a three instead of a ten dollar bill came out first. But there was the ten too. What did it mean? She had kept her desk locked, and given the key to no one, except — Of course, there must be an exception; and now she remembered letting Walter have it the evening before "to borrow an envelope." She knew where the money came from now. The bill was marked simply, "For the heathen;" but it was not for the heathen that tears of joy came to her eyes as she guessed its history.

"Kate, you and Walter are a pair of geese," said Charlie the next evening.

"Why?"

"Why, here you've put all you had into the collection, and Walter half he had; and it's a fact, that, with all the rich men in our church, there wasn't another bill larger than a five in the box. And now I suppose you won't have a cent to lend a fellow for the next six months. I declare, it makes me hate the very name of missions."

"Perhaps so; and yet if it were an American mother to be saved from the funeral-pile, — your own, for instance, — or Minnie from the alligators' jaws, you would not hate the name."

"Those alligators did service for missions in our hymns and picture-books twenty years after they had digested their last baby; but they are played out now. I suppose the funeral-fires must be used to kindle missionary zeal a while longer; but they haven't kindled any thing else for the past thirty years. And, now there's no such great work to be done, it seems to me folks might keep their money at home. I think the churches are beginning to look at it in that light."

"It were better the mothers had been left to throw them to the Ganges, than that, grown to be men, they should be offered by American Christians on the altar of the demon of covetousness."

"Such things never were done among the Buddhists, where your money has gone," said Charlie.

"So much the more chance for the money to do good, then," Katie answered.

"You have invested wisely," said Mrs. Bancroft. "I confess the story has a new interest to me, now we have reached the time when I began to give, and so to read missionary magazines as I would the reports of dividends from a bank where I was stockholder.

"The mission to Burmah had passed its infancy; a fact that involved several other serious facts, among them this, — that it is not an easy thing to cut the clothing of the growing youth from the same pattern that fitted his babyhood. When Judson was reading Pali, translating Matthew, and gathering, one by one, his eighteen converts at Rangoon, there were no native churches in the neighborhood clamoring for pastors; no schools looking to him for teachers; no Karen catechisms, geographies, histories, and trigonometries to be made; no tracts and Bibles begging to be printed; no untrained assistants, scattered far over the country, demanding all the time of an itinerating missionary to supplement their labors, and correct their blunders; no theological seminary, preparing teachers for those whom the schools were preparing to be hearers. His work, though hard, was simple. All this was changed now. Mr. Vinton had charge of a parish three or four times as large as all New England, with no railroads to take him from station to station; while a region of heathen Karens, three or four times larger, beyond, was begging him to come and bring them 'the white books.' Mr. Binney was professor of every thing in a seminary of theological students, — not the angels we often expect to find in converted heathen, but very imperfect saints, who growled about rations and accommodations, and taxed his patience by occasional frivolity, very much after the manner of some American students. Both these needed help, and so did many another. But the problem was, how to retain what help they had. To do this, the Maulmain Karen mission must have 6,041 rupees. It was allowed 4,146. No more could be expected from any quarter. All saw that something must be done; but no one dared to do it.

"At last Mr. Binney spoke: 'I move that the Sgau Karen boarding-school be dismissed, and the pupils be assisted, as far as may be, to return to Burmah Proper.'

"Dead silence followed. No one seconded the motion, and it was lost.

"He spoke again: 'I move that one-third of all the assistants in Burmah Proper, and one-fourth of all the other Karen assistants connected with this station, be dismissed from and after the first day of July next.'

"Another dead silence.

"He made a third motion, 'That the amount allowed to the theological seminary be reduced to five hundred rupees for the year 1848, and that the number of pupils and the period of study be adjusted to that amount.'

"Again no one spoke. The council of doctors, though convinced they could not take care of the whole of their patient, were unable to decide whether head, heart, or lungs, could best be dispensed with. At last they resolved to go on as they were, assuming the responsibility for the deficiency themselves, and appealing to the Board for help. Partial relief came, but not till after months of anxiety; and Maulmain was but a type of the rest.

"Time brought other than financial changes. In the earliest days of the mission the Karens were divided into two classes, — those who had decided to embrace Christianity, and those who had not. Now there were added two others, — those who had decided not to embrace it, and those who, having embraced it, had turned against it. Both these were usually either obstinately indifferent, or bitter opposers. A similar though less marked change was visible among the Burmans. 'I have heard your religion from the time of its first arrival in Maulmain, and I do not like it,' said one of them to Mr.

Mason. 'I have heard teacher Vinton talk a great deal, and I do not believe a word he says,' said a Karen to Mr. Moore. 'We have heard a great while, and do not want to hear any more,' said a company in another place to Mr. Brayton. The time when curiosity could be relied upon as an aid to Christianity was plainly past.

"And there were obstacles in the disciples themselves. In founding the mission, Judson did not have to meet the argument from the faults of professors; for there were none. Now it assailed the missionaries everywhere.

"There were church-members who were not converts: the converts were only converted sinners, and the most sincere of them were often ignorant.

"The Karens were a migratory people. Often a chapel would be built, and within two years left wholly alone; while those who worshipped in it were scattered far over the country. There the missionaries would sometimes find them, perhaps lights in the wilderness, guiding others to Christ; perhaps themselves led away into arrack-drinking and sabbath-breaking. Then they would repent and confess, break their arrack-bottles, and beg with tears to be taken back into the church, till the missionaries could hardly find heart to refuse; yet they always did refuse till the transgressors had proved their sincerity by their lives.

"New missionaries came,— in 1847 Mr. and Mrs. William Moore; a year later Mr. Benjamin, Mr. C. C. Moore, Mr. Van Meter, and their wives; in 1849 Messrs. Knapp and Campbell, with their wives, and Miss Wright; and in 1851 Mr. and Mrs. Thomas."

"It seems to me, that with sabbath-breaking, drunken disciples, obstinate heathen, cholera, small-pox, and short funds, the new missionaries had rather an uninviting prospect," said Katie.

"Fortunately for missions, they could not see what they were going to," remarked Clarence. "If a telescope could be invented, like the Yankee's gun with a bent barrel, made to shoot round corners, and the missionaries could see over or around the world's curve, into Burmah, before embarking, our story would probably be very much shortened."

"That's so," said Charlie. "But the disappointment must have been all the greater when they arrived."

"Yes," said Mrs. Bancroft. "When Mr. and Mrs. Thomas, after spending seven months in the city of Tavoy, went out into the jungle, they were disappointed indeed. Christian villages entertained them; they worshipped in Christian churches; they knelt in prayer in Christian families; they attended the meeting of an association where letters from seventeen churches were read, and native Christians framed and passed resolutions, and discussed questions of policy as appropriately as could many an association in America.

"'What has been accomplished,' Mrs. Thomas wrote, 'is far more important and extensive than I imagined in America. Truly the Lord has wrought wonders in this land. Many times, when I look at these assemblies of converted heathen, I think that all the sacrifices missionaries ever made are amply repaid.'

"Notwithstanding the grave faults of the converts, Mr. Moore, almost on his first arrival, could write, 'The line of distinction between church-members and the world is more plainly marked than at home. We seldom have to ask an individual whether he is a disciple: there is something in their countenance and deportment that distinguishes them.'

"The truth is, it will not do to judge the sun by its spots, especially as they would not seem dark but for the sunlight around them. And the Burman mission had its bright surface. A year made a great change in the Theological School: the frivolity and selfishness that had marked too many of its pupils were gone. Often, as they talked together of the sufferings of Christ, their faces would be averted to wipe away the tears; and questions would remain for minutes unanswered, because no one was willing to break the solemn silence of the room. Such a school could not help sending forth better pastors, and such pastors could not but train better churches.

"When Mr. Abbott went to America, he left in the region about Sandoway two ordained ministers and twenty native assistants, — most of them in Burmah Proper. The ordained pastors were Myat Kyau and Tway Poh, both rare men in zeal and in good judgment. Of the latter, Mr. Beecher wrote as follows a few years later: —

"'No native preacher has a greater or better influence abroad, and none is more beloved and respected at home. As we passed by or entered his room from day to day, and saw Tway Poh — the *Rev.* Tway Poh, we should say; for no minister was ever more worthy of the title than he — sitting by his table, reading and studying, or conversing with those who sought his advice, we often wished that our brethren and sisters who feel such an interest in this people could experience the delight that we did as the expression came involuntarily to our lips, "How much like a pastor in his study at home!"'

"Under such care the work went on. The pastors baptized more than a thousand in Mr. Abbott's absence; and, when he returned to the field in 1849, he could report an association of thirty-six churches with forty-five hundred members, as many as five thousand unbaptized Christians, and all supplied with the means of grace, and the churches so trained to self-support, that the whole cost the Union but little over three hundred dollars.

"The Christian village, Ougkyong, was rebuilt, in part, on a more healthy site; and Mr. Beecher, visiting it in 1851, reports an interesting covenant-meeting, six baptisms, and no cases needing discipline. 'Some of the members,' he says, 'had suffered annoyance by the neglect of others to watch their buffaloes, but had shown such Christian forbearance, that no difficulty arose.' Substitute hens or sheep for buffaloes, and suppose the church an American one, and you will see that this indicated no mean degree of growth in grace.

"But of the state of the mass of the Bassein converts through those years, tidings came only at rare intervals.

"On the 12th of April, 1850, Dr. Judson died on his way from Maulmain to the Isle of France. Thus ended thirty-seven years of labor for Christ. Going back to that country inn, where, all night, the powers of light and darkness struggled for the direction of his soul, then looking at Burmah to-day, with its translated Bible, its more than three hundred churches, its twenty thousand Christians, its ripened fruit gathered into the heavenly garner, and then thinking what would have been the result of that life if the decision of that night had been for infidelity, we tremble, and thank God.

"In 1851 Mr. Kincaid came back from America with Mr. Dawson, a physician. They went at once to Rangoon, but found themselves in the midst of a storm of opposition. Disciples had been fined and imprisoned; the natives were afraid, at any price, to rent houses to missionaries. The governor placed a spy over Mr. Kincaid, and forbade his entering a single house without this attendant. It was rumored that he was to be put in irons. His best friends dared not recognize him; and even the coolies in the street took pains to jostle him rudely. With much help from grace, and perhaps a little from nature, he was able to resist the tempest till the governor had time to write to Ava. Then there came an order from 'his Majesty, whose glory is like the rising sun, whose chiefs walk under golden umbrellas, the King of elephants, and Lord of many white elephants,' that 'the American teachers should be allowed, if they wished, and at any time they might choose, to come up to the golden feet; or, if they preferred to remain at Rangoon, they were not to be molested.'

"The change was instantaneous. Insolence gave place to profound respect. Visitors crowded the house. Mr. Kincaid preached to them openly and fearlessly, as if in America: and soon the people had a chance to stare at the golden umbrellas, that mark a priest of highest rank, going to and from the house of the missionaries; for the king's alchemist and astrologer from Ava had taken up his quarters with him, saying he 'could not feel easy anywhere else.' Even the governor was civil; and once, when passing through his audience-room, Mr. Kincaid was asked the question, 'Are you one of Jesus Christ's men?' He answered, 'Yes, and I will give you the reason;' and for nearly half an hour preached, unmolested, to the company of thirty gathered there.

"Of the eighteen baptized by Mr. Judson during his first stay in Rangoon, two lived to welcome the new missionaries, — Mah Mee and the old pastor Ko Thah-a. Both were over eighty. When, in 1832, Moung Thah-a knelt before Mr. Judson, and, with folded hands, reverently begged for baptism, neither of them dreamed that he was to be for thirty years, and through fiery trials, the shepherd and strength of the hunted Rangoon flock.

"'The teachers have come and gone,' he said. 'I have always remained here. When the teachers left Rangoon, the rulers seized me. They commanded me not to preach. They said, "Do you intend to preach Jesus Christ?" I said to the rulers, " I shall preach: Jesus Christ is the true God." '

"He had been imprisoned, fined, put in stocks, and swung up by the feet, for preaching Christ, and was well prepared to welcome new laborers into the field he was now too infirm to till. Soon the Karens of the towns around caught the news, and came in to see if the teacher had indeed come. This was not approved. In fact, in one case the governor told Mr. Kincaid, as coolly as he would have spoken of eating his dinner, that, if it continued, he should be under the necessity of shooting every Karen that came to his house, except the lame, the sick, and the blind. These he dared not prohibit; for Dr. Dawson's medical services had already proved too valuable to be interfered with. Still inquirers multiplied, and converts from both Karens and Burmans were added.

"One morning, about six months from the time Mr. Kincaid reached Rangoon, there appeared at the mouth of the river a fifty-gun ship and two armed steamers,— not a very alarming sight in itself to the governor, one would think. But the ghosts of murdered British subjects haunted him, and for a few days he was almost insane with terror. Perhaps, too, he was dimly conscious, that, for many months, the prayers of thousands of Christian Karens had been raising a battery against him, or had heard their words, 'We *know* that the day of deliverance is at hand;' for one of his first threats, when he had recovered from his fright, was, that, if the English attacked Rangoon, the Christian Karens should be placed in the front of the battle.

"Of course, the one ship and two steamers were not sent to fight the Burmans. Their object was to ask redress for outrages upon two British captains. Nevertheless, the long-looked-for deliverance had come. The redress was not given. Many other outrages became known to the commodore; and, in six weeks, war became almost a certainty. With great difficulty the missionaries succeeded in leaving with the British fleet. To have staid would have been certain death.

"Three months later, another fleet was thundering at the gates of the Burman Empire. Martaban fell on the 5th of April; Rangoon, on the 14th. Mr. Kincaid had arrived the day before. Mr. Dawson came on the 18th; and in a few days they had cleared an old building of its idols and cobwebs, and were again receiving disciples, inquirers, and patients. On the 20th December, 1852, Pegu was declared a part of the domain of Great Britain.

"Long after Rangoon was as safe a residence as London, the interior was a scene of terror. Bands from the disorganized Burman army were prowling, burning, and shooting, as they went over the country. The Karens organized to defend their homes. Almost daily, news of battle between them was brought to the missionaries at Sandoway. To the Burmans, all Christians were counted British sympathizers. Many were pierced with swords, beaten, or hung till almost dead, for being readers of the 'white book.' One aged pastor was crucified. Sixty of his flock were rescued by the British while *digging their own graves.*

"The Karens gave full proof of bravery, often driving back forces much larger than their own. 'I hear but one account of them,' wrote the commissioner of Pegu, 'that on all occasions their information has been the best, and their assistance the most hearty. We must not forget such good-will as has been shown us.'"

"But you haven't told a word about Miss Macomber," said grandpa Sears, "how she went out alone among those drunken Pwo Karens of Douggahn, and sometimes there wasn't a house for miles that would let her in; and they set fire over and over to the house she lived in. And she staid there three years, till there were twenty-six Christians, and then died. And how Knapp tried to live among the Nagas; and how we sent out the Haswells and Ingalls and Braytons and Bullards and Ranneys and Crosses."

"I wish I had time to tell it *all*," said Mrs. Bancroft. "You certainly must not judge the comparative importance of the work done by the amount of time I give to the separate workers; for there are many whose record is bright on the book above, but whose own labors, with their results, can hardly be separated from those of their brethren. But you shall hear from some of those grandpa has mentioned before long."

CHAPTER X.

NEW FIELDS. — TOUNGOO, SHWAYGYEEN, HENTHADA.

WHEN the thought of becoming a missionary first presented itself to Ida, it received very decided treatment as an intruder. The idea of becoming a cannibal would hardly have seemed more unnatural. But thoughts, like young robins, do not often make their appearance, except where nests have been made ready for them; and this thought, when it had forced its way into her mind and claimed a right there, found that through the months, undreamed by her, a nest had been preparing for it so exactly fitted to it, that, in less than two days, it was entirely at home.

Yet it did not seem to Ida that she had changed so much, but rather that this was the work for which she had been made, only she had failed, until lately, to understand herself. With this self-revelation came a consciousness that something more than natural fitness for the work was needed, a something that she had not; and so, through weeks of silent, anxious conflict, her purpose lay, as she supposed, hid in her own breast. At last she was able to write in her journal, "I do desire earnestly to do God's work, where he pleases, when he pleases, as he pleases."

That evening she announced her plan to the family.

"I think I shall offer myself as a missionary."

"I supposed so," said Walter.

"You have not written yet, then?" asked Mrs. Bancroft.

A moment's pause; and Katie added, "To what place?"

What did it mean? It had cost her months of preparation, and weeks of conflict, to be able to speak those words; and the family received them as they would an announcement that she was going to a tea-party. If she had felt any desire to make a sensation, she would have been indignant. As it was, she was relieved, but a little disappointed.

"Mother bought an extra piece of cloth for you last week, so she could be making it up for you, because you were going," said Edith.

"But I did not know I was going myself till yesterday, if I am," said Ida.

"I supposed not; but mother did: she knows the most always."

"I have felt sure of it for a long time, Ida," said Mrs. Bancroft. "But I could not be thankful for it at first: I am now."

Tears filled Ida's eyes. They did not misunderstand her, then, but had known her better than she knew herself instead.

"We are ready for the story, mother," said Walter. "Ida is impatient to hear about her future neighbors."

"The Burman emperor was lord of land and water no longer: his last inch of sea-coast had been taken. Rangoon, witness to the torture of so many British subjects, was itself British territory. Bassein — the home of Karen heroes and martyrs, into which Abbott had cast so many longing glances, and from which he had received so many hundreds to study, to be baptized, often to die — now lay open to the reapers; and farther north lay other regions, which might be inhabited by owls or Nats, for aught any white man could tell.

"From the borders of one of these darker regions a voice had come three years before the war. Sau Dumoo, a Karen living in Toungoo, had wandered down to Tavoy. There he became converted, entered the Theological School, and now was eager to go back and teach his countrymen.

"'There are many more Karens there than here,' he said, 'and they do not wander about as they do here. A man will build his house; and, when his daughter marries, she takes her husband to her father's house, or rather adds a little to the old house. This continues many years, till a few of these houses make a large community.'

"Sau Quala was intensely interested, and eager to go with Sau Dumoo to explore these unknown regions. At the meeting of the association in 1852, they together presented a request for leave to go as missionaries to Toungoo. There was a difficulty. The churches about Mergui looked upon Sau Quala as a father, and claimed the rights of children. They had heard of his intention, and sent to the association a protest, signed by every one of the assistants south of Tavoy, and by their churches. What was to be done? No other was so well fitted for Toungoo, or so much needed at home, as Sau Quala. 'We looked at the subject carefully,' writes Mr. Thomas; 'we spoke; we wept; we prayed; and all — the very men who had signed the adverse memorial — arose with tears, and *voted to approve his going.*'

"Sickness and war, still raging in Toungoo, delayed his going for a year. In September, 1853, Dr. and Mrs. Mason went there.

"'I consider it a fixed fact that you cannot go to Toungoo; no amount of preparation would take you there alive,' were the encouraging words of a letter received by Dr. Mason the day of his appointment to that field. The war was over; but bands of *dacoits* — a class of robbers who are by turns petted, tolerated, or cut in pieces, according to the interest of the Burman king — infested river and country.

"Nineteen days' travel through regions bristling with reports of men murdered, and villages robbed, brought the Masons within the walls of Toungoo city. It was mainly Burman; but around it were Khyens and Shans, and Karens of every sort. Here were Sgaus, like their kinsmen in Tavoy, repeating traditions of God's book, and waiting the coming of the white foreigners; Pwos, more reserved and more Buddhistic; Karennees, or Red Karens, named from the color of their garments, — a new tribe, wholly distinct from both Sgaus and Pwos; the pant-wearing Bghais, from whom even Burman avarice had never collected taxes, for the reason that no Burman entering their villages ever came out alive, and to whom kidnapping and murder were lawful avocations; the Taubya, or dog-eating Karens, named from their diet, diminutive in size and mind; the gentler frock-wearing Bghais; the Pakus; and, closely allied to or included in these, innumerable smaller clans, some of them almost own cousins, and separated not half a day's journey from each other, yet wholly unable to understand each other, so rapidly does language run wild when not trammelled by books.

"Dr. Mason had already been ordered to America by his physician when he started for Toungoo. He could delay no longer. In December, Sau Quala came; in January, 1854, Dr. and Mrs. Mason left.

"And now Sau Quala was left, aided only by a handful of unordained assistants, to plant and cultivate the Toungoo mission. Almost immediately many of the Karens were clamorous for teachers. He stationed Shapau at Hteedu, a Bghai village.

"'Let us have a teacher,' said the people of Theghadeu as they came with presents of salt and eggs to Sau Quala.

"'But I have but one, and I wish to leave him at Hteedu. Send some from your village to study here; and, when they can read, you may teach each other,' said Sau Quala.

"'But let him come to us. We will become Christians, and we will support him better than the people of Hteedu.'

"So they argued for a whole day and night; till Sau Quala said, 'I will leave teacher Shapau to stay one month at Hteedu, and then another month at Theghadeu, and so on each alternate month.' This satisfied them.

"Some of the Pakus were less cordial.

"'Let one of the teachers come up here,' said the chief of one of their villages, 'and we will make two or three holes through him with our spears; and, if he does not die, we will believe him, and worship his God.'

"On hearing this, an assistant set out at once for their village.

"'I heard you were going to pierce me with your spears,' he said. 'I am here now: if you wish to pierce, pierce. I trust in God, and have come to preach his words.' They were dumb; listened attentively; and he left unharmed. Soon two teachers were sent them.

"Sau Quala labored incessantly. He made long tours among the mountains, often prostrated by fever, sometimes poisoned by insects or strange plants, threatened by death in almost every form, but having no thought of rest while he had strength to work, or of discouragement when there was work to be done. His wife and child were sick, and he longed to see them. His father-in-law died; but he could not afford a visit home. The British commissioner offered him thirty rupees per month to act as overseer among the Bghais, Pakus, and wild Karens.

"'I cannot do that,' he replied; 'I cannot do that *at all.* I have no use whatever for the money. There are others to do this thing: employ them. As for me, I will continue in the work in which I am engaged.'

"'How do you get your support? Why do

you not want money?' asked the commissioner. 'We will give you money, and you can still be a teacher. Will not this be easy for you?'

"'No, my lord,' answered Sau Quala: 'I eat my food with poor people, and am content. I did not leave my beloved wife and child, and come to this distant place, to get money and eat delicious food: I came to preach the gospel to the poor, that they may be saved. If I perform the duties of a *n'kau* (superintendent), these wild Karens will become my enemies.'

"'Think upon the subject two or three days before you decide finally,' said the commissioner.

"Sau Quala *thought;* found two Christian headmen to take the place; and, greatly relieved, went on with his unpaid work as before.

"Within twenty-one months from that time he baptized one thousand eight hundred and sixty persons; yet his journal shows even greater caution in examining candidates than was common among white missionaries. Here there are 'several applicants;' but none are received, because they 'are recent converts.' There, out of a large number, two are admitted; in the next place nineteen; in the next none; for they 'had changed their teacher, so there were no

BIRTHPLACE OF QUALA, WHO BAPTIZED 1860 CONVERTS, AND ORGANIZED 28 CHURCHES, IN 18 MONTHS. IN THE TAVOY DISTRICT.

satisfactory means of knowing the state of their minds;' and some of the women, finding their fowls killed by children, 'had been so provoked as to sin with their lips.' And in the next, again, none; for their old feuds were not wholly given up. In the next, twenty-four out of eighty were received; the rest postponed 'on account of ignorance.' None were admitted to baptism without several distinct examinations at distant times.

"When Dr. Mason returned in 1857, he found, in the region which he had left utterly dark, two associations of churches, ninety-five preaching-stations, and twenty-six hundred baptized Christians, besides many more unbaptized. Among the Bghais, feuds which had separated their villages farther from each other than from America, making it death for a resident of one to enter another, melted away into friendship. Footpaths were made between them. The thirst for arrack gave place to the thirst for books. They built their own chapels, supported their own schools, and gave liberally to the work beyond. Their young men went everywhere, preaching,— for, among the Karens, a man no more requires a license to preach than to pray,

— living upon the poorest fare; sometimes working as coolies a part of the time, that they might have funds to preach the remainder. Nothing surprised Dr. Mason more than the number, talent, and familiarity with Scripture, of these suddenly raised-up native preachers.

"'When I stand on these mountain-tops,' he writes, 'and see now two, anon three, and then five clusters of Christian habitations, I feel, like the Queen of Sheba, "the half was not told." I could not convey to a congregation in America an adequate conception, that would be credited, of the magnitude of the work effected. Were the Union to become bankrupt, and all the missionaries to return home, it would go on without our aid as certainly as the dawn increases to the perfect day.'

"On one occasion, a company of young British officers rambled out into the Toungoo jungle for pleasure, and returned, pronouncing the Karen Christians 'hypocrites.' They had reached one of their villages on Sunday, and found it impossible by any effort to hire a boat till the next morning.

"'Is that all?' asked a pious officer. 'Was there nothing else wrong in their conduct, except that they refused to let their boat on Sunday?'

"'Why, no,' was the constrained admission. Both boat and men were ready to serve them on Monday morning.

"'Then they were only consistent,' said the brigadier.

"Indeed, none appreciated the wonderful change more than the government-officers, and through them liberal aid was obtained for the schools.

"'The commissioner seems about as great an enthusiast as you deem me,' writes Dr. Mason after a visit from Major Phayre. 'He remarked at parting, "I can assure you I came with high anticipations; but I have been truly surprised at what I have seen."'

"Mr. Whitaker came from Maulmain a few months before Dr. Mason arrived; labored in Toungoo, surrounded sometimes by hundreds of eager listeners, for two years; and then died, rejoicing that God had brought him to Burmah to see what he had seen.

"Among the Bghais, 'wildest of the wild,' there were, at the close of 1861, nearly two thousand members. Mr. Cross, who had joined the mission nearly two years before, writes of attending an association among them, more quiet and orderly than any three or four days' camp-meeting in America; and well asks, 'Why were these thousand or more of wild Bghais now so sober, so orderly, so intent on hearing rebukes of sin, and exhortations to honesty, justice, and holiness?' The whole number of church-members in Toungoo was at that time four thousand seven hundred and thirty-three; but they represented a Christian population of twenty thousand.

"But now a dark cloud came over Toungoo. The Christian Karens found themselves suddenly in the midst of a war between the British government and a heathen chief. Their villages were burned, their women and children carried into slavery, their schools broken up, their fields abandoned for the camp.

"The contest was short; but, before its smoke had cleared away, the infant churches were called to a far more perilous spiritual conflict. Mrs. Mason, partially deranged in mind, imagined that there had been revealed to her a new language, written in the figure of the carpet, in the lines of the human face, in the symbols of the

Buddhist religion, and in almost every object in nature, — a language which men needed only to learn in order to become Christians; which the heathen needed only to learn, to see that they were already worshipping the true God. By it she could read the doctrine of the Trinity in the form of the Buddhist pagoda, and the New Testament in Karen dresses and sacks. To teach it to the world she now considered her great mission.

"The Karens knew nothing of the refined forms of monomania peculiar to civilized countries. To them, one who was not crazy was sane. In Toungoo, as in America, there are two classes of church-members, — those who study the Bible for themselves, and those who accept the interpretation of it given them by their teachers. To many of the latter class the new 'God language' seemed a revelation fresh from heaven. I sometimes wonder what the Galatian church would have done if the terrible hypothesis of the apostle — 'If I, or an angel from heaven, teach any other gospel' — had become a reality; how many of them, when called to choose between Christ and him who had taught them Christ, would have chosen rightly.

It seems less strange, that, in a like trial, many of the Karens failed, than that a majority of them still held the old faith; but it was only a majority.

"Directed by Mrs. Mason, the accepters of the God language refused Sau Quala, and the other preachers who rejected it, admission to their pulpits, or even to their houses. Churches were divided; schools were given up; and heathen villages on the point of turning to Christianity looked at this new development, paused, and turned back. At last an entire separation was thought necessary. A new association was formed among the Pakus, and another among the Bghais. In 1865 the connection of Dr. and Mrs. Mason with the Missionary Union closed.

"It is easier to break than to mend is more terribly true among spiritual things than among temporal. In the years that followed, through the efforts of the missionaries, now and then an individual, a pastor, sometimes a church, saw its error, and repented; and the faithful native pastors gathered fresh energy from the trial, and went out as in the early times when the contest was only with heathenism. The Karens who held to the old faith realized as never before the necessity of Bible study; and Sunday schools were everywhere organized. In 1867 we begin to hear again, now of one hundred and eighteen baptized by one preacher on a tour, and, soon after, one hundred and twenty-six by another; then of a teacher going alone to a village that seemed a mere nest of writhing vipers, and working till they were 'among the kindest-acting and most pleasant-looking people in the mountains.' But these cases were exceptions. Division of feeling and interest among believers would not bear a different fruit in Toungoo from that which comes from the same tree when planted in America; and for some years revivals hardly kept pace with declensions; the interest in the jungle schools slackened; many of the native preachers lost their early zeal, and discipline was neglected.

"In 1869 there came the first convert from the Red Karens. For months he had believed, but feared to profess it, lest, going back among his countrymen, he should yield to temptation, and dishonor Christ.

"'Teacher,' he said with tears in his eyes the evening before his baptism, 'I have asked baptism: I want you all to pray for me.'

"And then, as one after another, visitors from his own people, came in, he told them his story, and met only laughter.

"'Oh, how dark my people are!' he said: 'they know nothing but darkness.'

"But, just before his baptism, there came a letter from his wife; 'Study hard, and do not fear for me. If you can, come home in the dry season, and help me get my rice; but do not come until you have learned all. I, too, am resolved to leave off evil, and do right.'

"Soon we find him laboring earnestly among his people. Eleven of them have since been baptized; and S'au, their pioneer missionary, has within the past year (1876) been ordained.

"In 1871, Dr. Mason, who for many months had been laboring to restore harmony to the churches, became again a missionary of the Union.

"'If there is to be peace, we will repair our chapel, and again support our teacher,' was the comment of more than one wounded and withering church.

"In January, 1872, came the brightest day Toungoo had known for years. The two Bghai associations came joyfully, cordially, and thoroughly together; and I think among the angels was as glad a song of triumph that day as when, seventeen years before, they greeted the entrance of the first Toungoo converts into the heavenly kingdom.

"The work of re-union proceeded more gradually among the Pakus; but by February, 1873, Mr. Cross was able to write, —

"'There are now but few churches that follow Mrs. Mason; and it is safe to say, that all that do follow her do so as a mark of their apostasy, or return to heathenism.'

"In 1874 Dr. Mason finished his work on earth, but not till he had seen, as the result of the union of his own labors with those of Dr. Cross and Mr. Bunker, fifteen new preachers located, a dozen chapels built or rebuilt, a spirit of work unknown for years stirring among the disciples, and a spirit of inquiry (also long unknown) enkindled among the heathen.

"During that year and the next, the whole field suffered greatly from famine. Vast armies of rats swept, three or four times in succession, over fields that had supported twenty thousand Karens, often destroying a whole field in a night. Among the heathen, hundreds died of starvation; and the Christians suffered much, and were greatly scattered.

"Mr. and Mrs. Crumb joined the mission early in 1877. Mr. Bunker has just completed a thorough re-organization of the Bghai churches. They now number 2,068 members, and the Pakus 1,843.

"Sau Dumoo, who first interested Sau Quala in Toungoo, was sowing and reaping at once in a neighboring field. At

SHWAYGYEEN

Mr. Harris commenced a mission to the Karens in 1853. In the first year of the mission five hundred and seventy-seven were baptized, five hundred of them by Sau Dumoo; and by 1860 the Shwaygyeen Association numbered more than twelve hundred members. But the station proved sickly. Mrs. Harris died very soon after reaching it. In 1856 Mr. Harris's health failed; Mrs. Miranda Vinton Harris, his second wife, and one of the most successful missionaries, died; and he left the mission, and in 1858 closed his connection with the Union. Mr. Watrous's health soon failed, and for six years Shwaygyeen was left without a missionary. The state of the sheep thus left in the wilderness is best described by one of their own pastors, writing in 1865 : —

"BELOVED BRETHREN OF OTHER COUNTRIES AND CITIES, IN EVERY PLACE, — I desire to write you a few words about the disciples of Christ in Shwaygyeen. To every one who may see this letter we would say, Bear with us, and pray to God, our Lord, for us; for we here in Shwaygyeen have no missionary teacher to instruct, encourage, or help us, as they have in other places.

"We are like orphans, — bereft of father and mother; left desolate, sleepy, and hungry: in other words, we are like the wounded and fallen, without a physician. The reason of sorrow is this. During the year some have apostatized from the living God, and returned to the customs of their forefathers; some have become unstable, and are wavering and restless, like the waves of the sea: therefore, beloved brethren in every place, bear with us, and help us by your prayers. Teacher Cross of Toungoo does all he can for us; and through him we receive New Testaments and hymn-books.

"During the year 1865 we have been consulting how to get back our beloved teacher Harris from America. We, the disciples of Shwaygyeen, have collected two hundred rupees toward paying the passage of teacher Harris. Therefore, dear brethren and sisters in every place, great and small, male and female, have pity upon us, pray for us, and assist us to get back our teacher.

"(Signed)   "TEACHER PAH MOO."

"Of course Mr. Harris was re-appointed, and went; and, though Shwaygyeen had shared largely the sufferings of her twin-sister in the north, when he arrived there (in 1866) he found its churches all 'righted up once more, and taking the Bible only as their guide.'

"Mr. Harris worked on, with no white assistant except his wife, for eight years. In 1870 Sau Dumoo, his closest companion, died. The next year the failure of Mrs. Harris's health compelled her to leave, and he was for a time quite alone. But the pastors proved true assistants, and of their own accord proposed raising a fund, above all ordinary contributions, which should make them independent of foreign aid, except specific donations. In 1872 Kah Cher, a young Karen who had just graduated at Madison University, joined the mission; and, at the close of 1874, Mr. and Mrs. Hale arrived as missionaries to the Burmans of Shwaygyeen. There are now eight hundred and sixteen Karen church-members.

HENTHADA.

"Henthada, a hundred and twenty miles above Rangoon, was not unlike Toungoo. Here, in 1854, Mr. Thomas looked over an apparently unbroken waste of heathenism, asking, '*Can* any thing turn this mass of mind to the truth?'

"Very soon visitors flocked in, inquiring for the 'lost books.' A few weeks later, Mr. Thomas found three who were already Christians. They had been baptized ten years before by Aupaw, a teacher sent out by Mr. Abbott. They took Mr. Thomas to their house, showed him their little library, — a catechism, an old worn hymn-book, and a few New-Testament leaves,— and then brought to him two other families, eight in all, whom they had led to Christ. These eight were baptized. There was no house large enough to hold even that little church : so they celebrated their first communion under a buffalo-shed. Mr. Thomas prayed earnestly that 'the little one might become a thousand.' At the close of 1856 his prayer was half answered : it had become five hundred. The ingathering had not been rapid as in Toungoo ; but the foundations had been strongly laid.

"Then, again, the cry for retrenchment echoed through all the outposts in Burmah. Funds from America had failed. There was no money to build the house which Mr. Thomas must have in order to live in Henthada. It was intimated that he might be obliged to return to Maulmain.

"'Tell the disciples of Jesus,' Mr. Thomas replied, 'if they cannot afford me five hundred dollars to build me a house, I must, nevertheless, remain here, though it cost me my life. Yes, I would rather occupy a Karen house than leave my field of labor. I came to preach the gospel to the heathen, and my brethren at home promised to support me here. I spend my life as I agreed to do, with or without their support.'

"The work grew more rapidly now: the demand for teachers and preachers was constant. Mr. Thomas could no longer wait to have them educated, but sent them out almost as soon as they could say, 'Believe on the Lord Jesus Christ, and thou shalt be saved;' and the gospel news found new channels for itself daily.

"Once, as Mr. Thomas was sailing up the Irrawadi toward the place where he planted the first little church, he heard strains of music. It was the tune of 'Happy Land,' and the words were

'Yay Shu quai plah pa Shu dai boh.'
('Jesus pardons all our sins.')

Strange words for so wild a place. He turned in the direction of the music. A young Karen mother was singing the hymn as a lullaby. Yes; and all through Henthada he knew there were Christian mothers singing their children to sleep with gospel hymns. It was no time to leave. On another tour within the limits of Bassein he found an aged saint, 'unusually cleanly in appearance, and heavenly-minded,' the wife of the first convert and apostle among the Karens,—Ko Thah-byu. Mergui, Tavoy, Maulmain, Rangoon, and Arracan, all spoke to him through her, and forbade his abandoning Henthada.

"And there was no retrenchment, nor need of any, though the regular supplies almost failed; for God sent especial help. One hundred rupees came from England; eleven hundred from cities in Bengal, whose streets were yet red with the blood of the Sepoy war. Funds came from unknown friends in America, and from British officers in Burmah, and from the heathen even, and liberal offerings from the native Christians.

"In 1860 Mr. Thomas received a communication from the British deputy commissioner of

Henthada, always kind and liberal, in regard to a petition he had received, asking exemption from taxation for thirty-four men claiming to be Christian teachers in Henthada. It greatly puzzled him; for he could not imagine there was really any such number of *bona fide* teachers in a mission that had sprung up under his own eyes. How many hours per day did these men teach? what else did they do? who supported them? Mr. Thomas assured him that there were more than thirty-four Christian teachers in Henthada; that these had no other employment; that they were supported mainly by Christian Karens in the district, but partly by friends in America, and British residents in Burmah, among whom *the deputy commissioner of Henthada stood the most prominent.*

"Three years later he could report seventy-five preachers, and a membership of eighteen hundred, supporting their own schools, and nearly all their own preachers; and 1866 brought news of deeper interest, and marked revivals in many of the churches.

"Early in 1866 Mr. Thomas left Henthada for America. On reaching Rangoon, he learned that the departure of Mr. Beecher — who had been laboring there, not in connection with the Union — had left the Sgau Karens of Bassein without a missionary. The call was loud for *some one*. Mr. Thomas, knowing that he perilled his life by the delay, but hoping even so slight a change might restore health, accepted it, but was obliged to leave after one year, and reached America only to die there.

"Mr. D. A. W. Smith succeeded him in Henthada. His first work was a tour among the churches. At Kyantmau, as he was walking in the gray twilight, he was startled by a shrill exclamation: 'So you have not deserted us, teacher, though God has.' It came from an old woman approaching.

"'Oh! do not say so, aunt. What do you mean?'

"'During the rains one died, and another, and then another, and now my neighbor's grown-up daughter. If God loved us, he would not afflict us so.'

"The whole village had been troubled by the thought; and a whisper had spread among them, that, for such as died suddenly, there was no hope. Trembling, they asked, 'Is this true?'

"It was worth a long journey to see the light

that spread from face to face as one after another caught from the missionary the thought that trials are a *proof* of love,— God's costliest gifts.

"Farther on, a mother lay dying. Her son, Shway Lay, was at the seminary in Rangoon.

"'Do not let him know of my illness; it would intefere with his studies,' she said.

"So, heroically, she passed away without the sight of her son.

"So weakness and strength alternate among the Karen Christians.

"A little later, Mr. Smith met Shway Lay at the association. It was now vacation.

"'Do you wish to go to your village to spend two or three months there?' asked Mr. Smith.

"'I would rather be sent to preach among the heathen.'

"Others expressed the same wish.

"'Look here, brother,' said the missionary to a native pastor: 'see what spirit is fostered at the seminary. These young men have been absent nine months; yet none of them wish to go home, except for a visit of a day or two, but choose rather to be sent here and there preaching to the heathen. What shall we do with them?'

"'Why, we must send them, of course, and raise the money at once.'

"'The six hundred rupees just given in by the churches might do.'

"'That indeed; but I want to do something special in answer to this special call.'

"By this time a group had gathered.

"'I will put down my name for five rupees,' said one.

"'And I three.'

"'And I two.'

"In a few minutes sixty-five rupees had been raised.

"'Can we not have a weekly contribution of a pice each from the church-members? A pice is so small, that they could do that without giving the less in the regular contributions,' proposed one of the disciples a year or two later.

"That year, their regular contributions for schools, chapels, and kindred objects, had been 4,981 rupees. The next year, the pice system alone brought in five hundred rupees.

"Mrs. Thomas returned in 1874, and has ever since been engaged with intense earnestness in rekindling the missionary spirit of the Henthada Karen churches, and arousing their pastors to direct evangelistic work among the heathen.

"Meanwhile Mr. Crawley, and, after him, Mr. Douglass, had been doing the slower work of a Burman missionary, talking daily to companies of men, — who would gather, and listen all day to religious discussions as to a theatrical exhibition, — and gathering converts one by one.

"In 1870 Mr. and Mrs. George arrived from America. This, when they had learned the language, left Mr. Crawley free for work in the jungle.

"Repeated tours were made. Every village where there was a Christian was visited, besides many where there were none; and in 1872 the result appeared in forty-one baptisms from among the Burmans, — a larger number than had ever been received in one year before.

"In 1875, though both missionaries were laid aside a great part of the time by sickness, there came a revival such as the Burman mission of Henthada had never known.

"In a region scarcely visited by the missionary, Mr. George found himself surrounded by loving converts, who insisted upon dismissing the hired coolies, and themselves transporting the baggage to its destination. Here, with insatiable eagerness, they busied themselves from morning till night in studying the Bible, and learning to sing Christian hymns. Few of them had ever heard a sermon; but they had read tracts; and several of them had witnessed a baptism, and dated their serious impressions from that. Within a year, more than one hundred were baptized. · The interest continues; and Mr. and Mrs. George have changed their home, that they might be nearer this great work, thus starting the new station of Zeegong.

"Mr. Crawley died near the close of 1876: so that the Burman work at the original station of Henthada is wholly in the care of Mrs. Bailey and Miss Payne, missionaries, of the Woman's Missionary Society."

CHAPTER XI.

RENEWED FIELDS.—RANGOON, BASSEIN, PROME.

THE next month was too busy to allow a single "missionary evening;" though, in one sense, all evenings were missionary evenings now. Ida's ideas in regard to her qualifications were far more humble than those of her friends. It sometimes seemed that it would take one lifetime to fit her to even begin the work of a missionary. Studies that she had rejected or neglected as useless now seemed important. Every thing seemed important, indeed. She was thankful that she was young yet; that life, for the most part, lay before her. One year she resolved to give to study; and, in order to do this, she must leave home at once.

So, for four weeks, Mrs Bancroft and Ida, and the sewing-machine, held long councils. Katie was as enthusiastic as if she had been going herself, and counted it a special privilege, when, in the intervals of work for the children and grandpa Sears and the family, she could gain an hour to sew for Ida. Walter never joined these family councils; he was not often in the sewing-room : but somehow, if there was a trunk-lock to be repaired, or the sewing-machine was refractory, or purchases were to be made a mile down town, he was always on hand.

Grandpa Sears was interested in every thing, even to ruffles and tatting; yet the children sometimes found him looking down into the depths of the unpacked trunk in a silent, meditative way, perhaps thinking of threescore others who had as hopefully prepared for the mission-work since his remembrance, and had been called up higher.

Charlie spent his daytimes at school, and his evenings with Clarence. He "hated packing and getting ready to go off always; but this was the pokiest packing he ever knew."

But all was done at last. They had gathered at the depot, watched the last steam-puff of the cars that carried Ida away float off among the hills, and realized, that, except for two short vacations, they could claim her no longer.

Then, when night gathered around them, they were glad to meet again in the sitting-room, and listen to Mrs. Bancroft.

"RANGOON,

the oldest mission-station, might be called a 'new field' almost as truly as Toungoo or Henthada. The city was rebuilt as if by magic, and within two months counted a population of thirty thousand. Mr. Vinton soon joined Mr. Kincaid. Native assistants were sent out into the neighboring towns; and within six months that wilderness blossomed, and bore the fruit of seventy-five converted Burmans and Karens, while every sabbath witnessed baptisms.

"But pestilence and famine followed in the track of war. All through the country, the poor little Karen shanties, that never held provisions for many days in advance, stretched their roofs over starving, dying inmates. But one day, among some of these perishing ones, there spread a rumor that there was rice at Teacher Vinton's. He had bought it at his own risk, and was selling it to Karens on credit, without security. It seemed too good to be believed. But any thing was better than *lying still* and dying: so, in companies and singly, they flocked in, till Teacher Vinton's seemed more like a commissariat than a mission-house. At first he sold to Christian Karens only; but, as the suffering grew greater, he asked no questions, and kept no account.

"'You are ruining yourself. These promises to pay will amount to nothing,' predicted his merchant-friends. They might well say so. He had spent nearly two thousand dollars; and the wildest American speculator would hardly have offered him as many cents for his investment. Yet, in time, every cent was paid, though not fully till years afterward. Long before that, Mr. Vinton had gained a better reward.

"'This teacher saved our lives; his religion must be worth having,' was the comment of the heathen. And so, wherever he went, they flocked around him, sometimes trying to worship him, always pointing him out to their children as their deliverer. In one year, more than seven hundred were baptized.

"At the same time, at the zayats in the city, companies of eagerly-listening Burmans gathered around Mr. Ingalls and Mr. Stevens, who preached incessantly; and every week there were baptisms.

"More were added in this one revival than had ever before, in the same length of time, been added to a Burman church.

"A year later, Mr. Ingalls found his health failing, and was warned to go to America.

"'I cannot leave,' was the answer, 'until some brother is ready to come and care for these souls as I have done.'

"Another year, and the sacrifice was complete. Mr. Ingalls died on March 14, 1856.

"Two weeks later, the old pastor, Ko-Thah-a, had joined him in heaven.

"Two years later, the disciples and missionaries gathered around the dying-bed of Mr. Vinton. Never before had the blows fallen so rapidly and heavily.

"A few months later, with Ko En and some other native assistants, Mrs. Ingalls was making a twenty-three-days' tour through the jungle, doing, in every thing except preaching, the work that her husband had left unfinished. And through the years that followed we find her, now visiting districts where no white woman had ever been seen, and talking to groups who crowded around her so closely she could hardly breathe; then sitting in the zayat of a Burman priest to encourage her assistants, who discussed with and silenced him; again visiting feeble churches, and directing inquirers, rejoicing in conversions, or mourning over apostates; then, for a while, making her home alone with the natives in one of those out-stations; and a few years later, when the church had grown to forty-five members, locating herself in a little shanty, a nest of snakes, scorpions, and many smaller creatures, and superintending the building of a chapel.

"Once she went as far as Bassein. On her way there, calling at a small village, she left her Burman girls to cook, and Mr. Crawley to preach to the priests, while she went into an idol temple to give books to the workmen, who were replastering some idols. A company collected.

"'I am the only one to testify for Christ,' Mrs. Ingalls thought; but from out the crowd there came a middle-aged man, who joined her in giving, with surprising accuracy, an account of the creation.

"'Who told you all this?' she asked.

"'Oh! I heard it many years ago from Teacher Ingalls. He told me all about the Lord Jesus

Christ, who came down to die for us; and I shall never forget it.'

"'Do you not know me?'

"'No.'

"'I am Mamma Ingalls.'

"Instantly the man clasped his hands, bowed low at her feet, and told her, that for years he had not worshipped idols; that he believed in the Eternal God, and wished to be his disciple.

"On one of her journeys by boat, just at midnight she reached a little Burman hamlet. The current was rapid; but they had promised to stop for an inquirer. Their call was answered. Torches were brought, and a group of listeners gathered about the canoe. Among them stood a noble-looking aged couple, the father and mother of the inquirer. Already they believed in the Eternal God, and Mrs. Ingalls talked to them of Christ.

"A few more visits, and the couple appeared with a band of candidates for baptism.

"'Where did you first learn about the Eternal God?' was asked.

"'In the golden city of Burmah's king, and from the white teacheress, whose husband was cast into the death-prison of Oung-pen-la. My husband took two books, and I carried rice and eggs to the beautiful white lady.'

"Did God have the conversion of those two in view when he sent Judson to Ava? And did sower and reaper — the 'white teacheress' of Ava and the white teacheress of Thongzai — rejoice together as the old lady, rising to receive the hand of fellowship, exclaimed, 'This is the happiest hour of my life; for I have found rest in a Saviour'? God knows.

"In 1863, on a jungle-trip from Thongzai, where she had removed, she met with a man who declared himself an opposer. In conversation with him, she chanced to mention the name of her preacher, — Moung Thah Dongnee, a native of the region.

"The opposer's countenance changed. 'Has that man embraced these as truths?' he asked.

"'Yes, and is now a teacher of them.'

"'You may talk to the rest: I shall come and hear from the lips of my friend.'

"The next day he came, and met Moung Thah Dongnee.

"'Do you know me?' he asked.

"'No.'

"But in a moment more tears started to the

preacher's eyes, and they were clasped in each other's arms.

"Then followed questions, and the story of their years of separation.

"'And now,' said Thah Dongnee, 'I must tell you the joyful news of salvation.'

"He began; and so deeply were they absorbed, that for a long time they puffed on with fireless cigars, much to the amusement of Mrs. Ingalls's other visitors. All night, till daybreak, Mrs. Ingalls could hear them talking and reading.

"'I think I believe,' was the morning salutation of the man, who, two days before, had been a bitter opposer.

"Almost immediately after Mrs. Ingalls removed to Thongzai, forty miles from Rangoon, a remarkable revival commenced, in which the native preachers — aided by Mr. Stevens of Rangoon and Mr. Crawley of Henthada — gathered a large number into the church. The same year a little church was organized at Letpadan, a day's journey distant. The gain was steady until 1864, when the beautiful chapel at Thongzai was burned to the ground. The church then numbered eighty-eight; but the heathen from the community, if heathen they could be called, gathered around the ruins, and mingled their tears with those of the Christians.

"'If you could wear yellow garments like mine, I could give you a hundred changes; and, if you could eat rice and our food, I could bring you loads of it before night,' said an old Buddhist priest as he gave Mrs. Ingalls a bowl, a mat, and some native cloth. And afterwards heathen vied with Christians in bringing dishes and cloth, and posts for the new chapel; and soon the work was going on as prosperously as ever.

"Miss Adams joined the Thongzai mission in 1868, but after two years removed to Henthada. Her place was filled early in 1872 by Miss Evans, the first missionary sent out by the Woman's Missionary Society. The organization was not a year old then: now it has under its care twenty-one missionaries, twenty-five Bible-women, and eighteen hundred and seventeen pupils in schools, distributed over nearly all parts of the foreign field.

"Let us look in for an hour, just now, upon these women at their work. Here, in the house of a Buddhist priest, seated, contrary to all rule, on a seat a little higher than his own, is a delicate young lady *repairing a clock*. She can talk little to him yet; but her work may prepare the way for a time when she can. Meanwhile she hands him her watch. It will preach to him maybe; for its hands will do what those of his idols cannot, — move.

"And now into Mrs. Ingalls's room came a company of heathen Burmans from a distance. 'Our idols are gods' is their steady reply to all her arguments.

"She quotes Scripture.

"'The teachers made the Scripture as they pleased,' is the answer.

"She takes out a German doll, and presses it. Of course, it adds the strength of its voice to the argument.

"'Your idols cannot even make a noise when pressed.'

"They look, then shake their heads. 'Our idols are gods,' they say, and withdraw to another room.

"Presently a Madras man comes in. He can speak only a few words of Burman. She knows nothing of his language. Perhaps, if she tries to amuse him, he will think more kindly of missionaries, and, when he goes home, listen more readily to those there; but is this all? Can there be no preaching without words? She takes a little idol, and places it before a paper of needles. Of course, nothing happens.

"She puts a magnet in its place. The man screams with wonder as he sees the needles shooting forward to meet it. He seizes it, examines it, and satisfies himself there is no trick.

"'English god!' he exclaims; and then, catching up needles, magnet, and idol, rushes into the room where the Burmans are now sitting. The idol is set before the needles.

"'Lohgeh!' ('Come!') says the Madras man; but the needles fail to obey.

"He tries the magnet. 'Lohgeh!' and instantly the needles are joined to it. 'No god, no god!' he says, throwing the idol contemptuously back. 'Little god, but no god, no god,' he adds, placing the magnet before the Burmans.

"'It has more power than our idols; perhaps it *is* an English god,' suggests one of them.

"'No,' says another: 'the English God lives up in the heavens. Perhaps he made this strange iron.'

"And now they are willing listeners, while Mrs. Ingalls talks till late into the night of the true God.

"'I mean to read this book you have given me; I will see if these things are false,' says one in leaving.

"Will he? Certainly never again will either idols, or the English God, be to any of that company what they have been.

"But Dea Thahlay is here now: let us listen while he tells his experience.

"'When I was a heathen, I bought a large idol made of light stuff, and very gaudy. One day I found some large holes in it. I performed my devotions, then pounded on it, and, behold! two or three large rats ran out. Then I was very angry, and said, "What! you a god, and not able to defend yourself from rats? Do I worship a god that cannot defend himself from rats?" I seized a club, laid him prostrate, and pounded him in pieces. The old priest came out, and exclaimed in horror, "Young man! what are you doing?" — "I am knocking to pieces my god, who cannot defend himself from rats," said I. I never bought another idol; and, when I heard the gospel, I rejoiced in it.'

"If all rats made equally good missionaries, probably American Christians could exercise self-denial enough to export a number sufficient to meet all demands.

"But to the true missionary, if only Christ be preached, it matters little whether the preacher be Bible, or clock, or doll, or magnet, or rats, or medicine-chest.

"Sometimes the stoniest ground bore choicest fruit.

"Once, late at night, Mr. Crawley, Mrs. Ingalls, and the native assistants, were passing though the village of Thay Bao. The Word had often been preached there, but with no visible result.

"The travellers were faint from their long walk, had lunched on dry salt fish, and were in need of water. They were refused.

"'What is the reason?' asked Mrs. Ingalls.

"'We have talked of your religion,' answered one of the women; 'and, as you say there is no merit from wells and water, I have told them to refuse water to Christians. We will feed dogs and crows, but not you.'

"'Will you lend us a rope and bucket?'

"'No.'

"At last one woman was persuaded to *sell* a small jar of water, and the missionaries passed on.

"Months passed by. The village — known

rather as 'the village that refused water to the mamma' than by its real name — was visited by cattle-plague and fire, and became the subject of earnest prayer among the Thongzai Christians.

"In 1872 one man from the place was converted; six months later there came a call for a visit, and native preachers were sent; and when, in 1873, Mrs. Ingalls visited them with her company, she was welcomed by a band of praying converts to the shelter of hospitable homes, and brought through the forest with songs of rejoicing.

"Before another year had passed, the once closed water-tanks had been given to the teachers, the monastery was converted into a chapel and schoolroom, and the Buddhist priest had become a Christian preacher.

"'This is not the work for two women, but for an army of strong men,' says Mrs. Ingalls as she sees, one after another, the Buddhist leaders joining the ranks of the secretly convinced, but shrinking from the next step which would place them among the open believers. But two women 'with God are a majority;' and in all the Burman mission there is no brighter spot than Thongzai.

"A like, yet very different work was Mrs. Vinton's. 'Will the mamma leave us?' was the first question of the Karen converts when Mr. Vinton died; and from outside the city disciples flocked in, begging her to stay, and pledging her their support.

"Two years before his death, Mr. Vinton, differing with the Board in regard to the extent of his control in the management of the mission, and believing that this difference affected interests vital to the success of his work, closed his connection with the Missionary Union. For similar reasons, Mr. Harris, Mr. Beecher, and Mr. Brayton, withdrew, and connected themselves with the Free Mission Society. Mr. Vinton relied for his support upon the Karens and the voluntary contributions of friends. Thus at his death Mrs. Vinton was left alone in charge of an independent mission of fifty churches, three thousand church-members, and numerous schools.

"'I well remember,' writes her daughter, '.that, at the semi-annual meetings of the Karen Home Mission Society, the native pastors and trustees used to come to her for advice in all matters connected with the mission, just as they used to come to my father; and they seemed to look up to her with the same reverence and love they had for him. Many times, as she sat in the centre of a group of pastors and teachers, have I heard them say, "When our father, Teacher Vinton, died, we felt like orphans: but this our mother did not forsake us; and had it not been for her, to go before us, and lead us on as Joshua did the Israelites after the death of Moses, surely we would not have been able to go forward."'

"When taunted by the heathen with having a woman for their head, they replied, 'She is our *mother*, and better to us, her poor children, than any two men; but by and by the son of his father is coming to us, and then you shall see.' The reference was to J. B. Vinton, then a student in America.

"During all this time she kept up a school of one hundred pupils, with a reputation such that a student had only to bring a certificate from her that he had been educated there, was a competent surveyor, and was trustworthy to be admitted to a situation in the survey under the British Government; and, at the close of the survey, the students would often bring in from two hundred to five hundred dollars each of their salaries to aid in carrying on the school; besides gifts to Mrs. Vinton and her daughter who assisted her.

"In 1861 'the son of his father' arrived, and was welcomed by the Karens as if he were their old teacher come to life again. In 1862 Mrs. Vinton and her daughter were compelled by ill health to leave for America. The close of six months of hard work, in which she travelled incessantly, frequently addressing large congregations, found her apparently much better; but the change was only in appearance. In 1864 she reached Rangoon, accompanied by her daughter and son-in-law (Mr. Luther), but came there only to die.

"Brainard Vinton did not disappoint his wild brethren. For six months of every year he made his home in the jungle, travelling almost constantly.

"'Where does Teacher Vinton live?' was sometimes asked of a Karen disciple.

"'*There*,' would be the answer, pointing to the elephant he rode.

"Mounted thus, and accompanied by his native preachers and some part of his brass band of seventeen trained musicians, he passed from village to village, systematically deploying his preachers right and left, expecting them not only to preach, but to make, each year, accurate observations that should serve as the basis of the next year's work. In this way the whole field was canvassed.

"All the confidence the Karens had given the father was transferred to the son. If a native was bitten by a poisonous serpent, Teacher Vinton must kill or capture the snake, and provide the remedy; if a man-eating tiger was about, Teacher Vinton must be sent for to destroy it. In fact, Teacher Vinton was the specific for all troubles, natural or spiritual. But through their confidence in him he trained them rapidly to self-dependence.

"Once he found a large congregation worshipping in a small, broken-down chapel. He preached a sermon on the text, 'Ye are not your own,' and closed by asking them to raise one hundred dollars for a new chapel.

"They were frightened. All saw the necessity for the chapel; but to raise the money *themselves* seemed quite impossible. They met again the second day. The third, as they were still deliberating, a sound was heard outside. In rushed a naked herd-boy with the cry, 'I've found an elk!' Instantly church and missionary were off on the chase. The missionary's shot brought down the elk. Strange to say, not a Karen had his knife with him.

"'Let us all take hold together, and we can carry him to the village as he is,' said Mr. Vinton, suiting action to word.

"They tried again and again, but in vain.

"'Then some of you boys go to the village and get knives.'

"It was done; and soon the elk was cut up, and each man carried his own part easily.

"'Hold there!' said one of the deacons: 'this elk has preached me a sermon. Do you remember how we lifted and tugged, and couldn't stir it, when we tried to lift it altogether? But, now it is cut up, we can carry it easily enough. Let us try that hundred dollars in the same way. What is my share, teacher?'

"Instantly Mr. Vinton made a mental assessment.

"'About ten dollars.'"

"'But *I can't* do as much as that,' said a poor disciple.

"'No: your share would be one rupee.'

"Before they parted, the whole sum was pledged.

"The next year, meeting them in their pleasant new chapel, he asked who of them had suffered from their liberality.

"Not one could say that he had had any thing the less to eat. They agreed that the Lord had more than paid them.

"A paper had been prepared, asking how much it would cost to give the chapel a shingled roof.

"'Hold on!' said the deacon: 'I'll give hoof and horns of that elk.'

"There was a laugh; but soon seven hundred dollars were raised for the shingling.

"That church gives seven hundred dollars annually now for religious purposes.

"In 1871 Mr. Vinton brought his band of twenty-five hundred well-trained Karens again into line with the forces of the Missionary Union. Since then, their number has increased to 3,311. They entirely support their own churches and schools, raising annually sixteen thousand rupees for that purpose.

"The school of barelegged theologians is a seminary now; but Dr. Binney is no longer professor of every thing. His cares are shared by D. A. W. Smith; and had we visited it at any time during 1876, while both these missionaries were in America, we should have found it still going on prosperously under the direction of the modest and indefatigable Sau Tay, whose sermons missionaries as well as heathen find profitable, and who is able, aided only by native assistants, to carry forward all branches of study pursued there.

"Not far away is the Rangoon College, under the care of Prof. Packer, founded in 1872, and now numbering more than one hundred students.

PROME,

about one hundred and seventy miles above Rangoon, was founded two or three centuries before the Christian era. The darkness of twenty centuries was first broken when the only white missionaries in Burmah were in the death-prison of Ava, the eighteen obscure disciples dispersed to meet no more on earth; and Moung Shway-Gnong alone, in Yatoung village, taught his neighbors the new truth he had found. Three years later, at the base of the towering gilded pagoda, Judson preached to

Mrs. Binney and her Sgau Karen School at Rangoon.

listening crowds, stirring the whole city for three months, till, at a whisper from the golden lips, congregations and inquirers became invisible together. Here, three years later still, Kincaid scattered tracts among eager hands, and rejoiced to find four who had 'believed ever since Teacher Judson was there.'

"It was one of the first stations occupied after the war. Coming here early in 1854, Mr. Kincaid and Mr. Simons found a native already on the ground, and active in preaching. Within two years, one hundred and fifty were baptized, principally Burmans: not all recent converts, however; for many seeds scattered in past years had grown up wholly untended, and were bearing fruit.

"There were fewer converts in the years that followed, but perhaps nowhere else so many from the classes usually called the hardest to reach. Here a Buddhist priest, who had fitted himself for his office by eight years of study, and would not even listen to the zayat preaching, was visited day by day by an earnest convert of eighty-four years, who came, leaning on his staff, to the kyoung, and preached Christ, until the priest, too, was a disciple. There a wealthy timber-merchant, a fine business-man, owning one of the best houses in Prome, after remaining for years an inquirer, surprised all by making an open profession; while in after-years Mr. Simons mentions receiving letters from early converts, whom for years he had wholly lost sight of, showing an earnest, mature piety.

"Mr. E. O. Stevens (son of Dr. Stevens of Rangoon) and his wife joined the mission in 1866. Soon after, a new church was organized at Enma. Five days later, while he was visiting a few scattered disciples at Poungdai, twelve miles distant, there came to him an inquirer. He had met him before, and had high hopes of him: now they were disappointed. He had decided that he could not give up all, and ask for baptism. The missionary led a little prayer-meeting, and then, sad and weary, lay down to rest. At sunrise we find him and his party wending their way — Indian file — through a narrow footpath out of the village. They have passed but a few rods, when a voice is heard out of the jungle-grass behind them. They halt, and the inquirer of the last evening stands before them. He is the picture of unrest, — not enough a Christian to apply for baptism, and too much one to be happy without.

"'Can you not wait one day longer, and so preach in town?'

"It is impossible. Mr. Stevens proposes prayer. They ascend the ladder of the chapel near by, and one after another prays for the hesitating disciple. His whole frame trembles, and the tears flow fast.

"'I have wholly renounced idolatry,' he says, 'and believe in the Eternal God, and the Saviour Jesus Christ; but I cannot bear to think of my wife leaving me, and taking our only child.'

"'The sun will soon be hot,' says the missionary, taking his hat and umbrella: 'we must leave at once. But remember, if you defer obedience thirty days, as you propose, you may find it thirty times more difficult.'

"'If that is the case, let it be done at once,' is the decided answer. From that moment, perfect peace seemed to hold possession of his soul. That evening he was baptized, and became a member of the Enma church; but, before a year had passed, Poungdai had a church of its own, with twenty members. The Prome mission now numbers two hundred and twenty-five. The death of Mr. Campbell, Mrs. Rose, and Mr. Knapp, and, three years later, of Mr. and Mrs. Satterlee, the removal through sickness of Mr. and Mrs. Moore, and the withdrawal of Mr. Rose, had left Akyab and Ramree destitute. In 1857 the Arracan mission closed. For its fruit we must turn to

BASSEIN.

" Here Mr. Van Meter came as soon as the field was open after the war. Left to themselves as they had been so much, and founded in part by men who had their instructions only at second or third hand from the missionaries, the theology of the Bassein churches was not the most systematic: still the missionary found much more to rejoice over than to mourn. They had an active Home Mission Society; and in 1855 Mr. Van Meter reports their contributions for the extension of Christianity as more than five thousand rupees.

"When the society met in 1858, its members found themselves in possession of an article common enough in Western Christian experience, but new to them, — a debt. Six new preachers were asking to be sent out. At first, there was a slight feeling of despondency. Fortunately, there were no more enlightened Christians present to suggest retrenchment; none to say, 'Appoint no new missionaries till the expenses are brought within your means.' They supposed it was their duty to honor whatever drafts the Lord might be pleased to make upon them. A brief conference, and then a vote was taken to appoint the whole six applicants. Another conference, and it was suggested that a subscription be made on the spot. All approved, and in a few minutes three hundred and forty-seven rupees were raised, — enough to pay the debt, and support the entire six missionaries three months.

"All joined in a season of thanksgiving and prayer.

"Mr. J. L. Douglass, the first missionary to the Burmans of Bassein, arrived in 1854. He had hardly learned the language, when there came to him, from three hundred miles away in Arracan, a Burman, who had 'heard there was a Burman missionary in Bassein.'

"'I heard Teacher Comstock preach in Arracan,' he said, 'but did not believe what I heard; but, after he died, I received tracts he wrote, and read them, and then remembered what I had heard. I prayed God to help me understand, and to forgive my sins; and I believe he has given me a new heart. Now I have come to learn more, and be baptized.'

"Within three weeks Mr. Douglass baptized him. Soon he began to talk about preaching. The missionary had been praying for an assistant every day for a year; but he dared not see in the new-comer an answer to his prayers, till he had sent him to Mr. Ingalls in Rangoon for examination.

"'I am much pleased with him, and think he would be of service to the cause,' was the word that came back.

"So Mr. Douglass engaged him, with no salary except his rice and clothing; and he proved to be 'a man of prayer, apt to teach, and well acquainted with the Bible.'

"Soon a small Burman church was gathered, which, after fifteen years of the slow, steady growth common to Burman churches, has now become five, with one hundred members.

"But the most marked work was among the Pwo Karens, usually far harder to reach than the Sgaus. In 1859 Mr. Douglass reports the turning of a village composed entirely of Pwos to Christianity, and the formation of a Pwo church of thirty-five. Three years later, Mr. Van Meter found in one place three entire families of Pwos, who had 'thrown away the bottle' (Karen idiom for becoming Christians); in another place he found nineteen, who, within a week, had decided for Christianity; and that year the majority of conversions from heathenism were among the Pwos.

"In 1867 the Bassein Christians celebrated their first Christmas, wondering much that they had never heard of the day before. The same year a temperance pledge was generally circulated; and, wholly of their own accord, the Karens extended it to cock-fighting, horse-racing, opium-eating, and all heathen practices. Singing in parts was introduced, and the art spread like wildfire. In 1868, at the Sgau Association, there was an ordination, with programme prepared, and exercises conducted throughout, by Karens, except that Mr. Van Meter was moderator of the council of examination. Both at this association and at the Pwo, more than a thousand were present, testing, but not overtaxing, the hospitality of the little villages where they met. The Sgau pastor alone accommodated eighty; and the Pwo deacon took two hundred and seventeen, and some others in proportion. Probably they were not all provided with French bedsteads and silver forks. In 1869 some of the churches kept, for the first time, the week of prayer; and fifty were baptized during the meetings. There was renewed interest in education. When Mr. Thomas went there, there were but fifty newspapers taken. A year later, there were three hundred. In 1865 there were not three thousand Karens in Bassein who could read. In 1868 there were eight thousand; and, though very poor, they supported wholly their schools and pastors.

"Mr. Carpenter came in November of that year. His first work was to draught plans for a new set of dormitory buildings, to take the place of the frail and now fast-decaying old ones. At the pastor's meeting in December, the plans were explained. They seemed very large.

"'Too grand and expensive for poor Karens,' they said.

"'But I only ask a contribution of one rupee from each member during the next three years, to be paid in instalments of four, six, or eight annas, as they may be able.'

"This looked more reasonable. At last they gave unanimous consent to the work.

"With them to pledge was to perform. Karens chose the choicest trees from the mountains; Karen elephants dragged them to the streams. They were cut and sawed on the mission compound; and within eighteen months three thousand rupees of Karen money were transformed into seven cottages, built all of the very best material, attractive to any eyes, but especially to those of the contributors. Within two years more the number had doubled.

"Thus the Bassein churches are steadily stepping forward to independence. Still we must not think our work done there. Independence is not the only necessary virtue. There are few, probably, who have not some time been startled by the immediate juxtaposition in the Epistles of texts such as, ' Lie not one to another, brethren,' 'Let him that stole steal no more,' 'Be sober,' with such as ' Meet to be partakers of the inheritance of the saints in light,' 'Fellow-citizens of the saints and of the household of God,' or 'Concerning brotherly love it is not necessary that I write unto you.' We see the same contrast still. There is hardly a chapter in any of Paul's epistles — from those glowing with joy at the triumphs of grace to those written 'even weeping' — that might not be addressed, almost *verbatim*, to some one of the Bassein churches to-day.

"Mr. Van Meter died in 1870, and Mrs. Van Meter a year later; leaving Mr. and Mrs. Goodell, recently arrived, alone among the Pwos."

CHAPTER XII.

TAVOY, MAULMAIN, AND THE SHANS.

"HAVE you noticed any change in Walter lately?" Mrs. Bancroft asked Charlie.

"Nothing: only he's given up wheels and levers, and taken to chemicals. That's because he's going to be a doctor, I suppose. Clarence thinks he has some talent that way."

From the bay-window, whose curtain concealed her, Kate listened earnestly to the conversation.

A look of disappointment was Mrs. Bancroft's only answer.

"Oh, in his talk, you mean!" Charlie added, seeing it. "I've noticed how he stands up for the missionaries, of course. That's because Clarence don't. I've heard Walter defend rattlesnakes when Clarence said he hated them."

Charlie walked away whistling, knowing he

had not been quite truthful, Mrs. Bancroft thinking she had been mistaken.

Katie only read in the words of both the very thing she had been longing to hear. Walter *was* different, then. Her impressions were not a mere reflection of her hopes, or of that one evening, weeks before, when he had honestly showed her himself. Mrs. Bancroft had noticed a difference; and she knew in spite of his denials, or rather from them, that Charlie had. What this difference was she hardly thought then.

"Have you selected your field yet, Dr. Walter?" asked Clarence that evening.

"I — what?"

For the first time, Clarence saw Walter a little embarrassed; and he enjoyed it, though he could not guess the cause.

"Your field as a physician, he means," said Charlie.

"Oh! I guess we are ready for the story, mother."

"Perhaps one of the fields I shall describe to-night will suit you," said Mrs. Bancroft.

"I do not know that there is any thing that can be increased in breadth without diminishing its thickness; that is, if no additions are made to it from without: and, during the years when the Union was winning its great victories in Toungoo and Henthada, there was no real increase in the working-force. Tavoy felt this most severely. Mr. Thomas, Mr. Cross, Mr. Allen, Mr. Colburn, labored here in turn. Often there was but one missionary; for the years from 1860 to 1864, not one; and all that time worms and weather were busy among the mission-buildings, and Satan and speculators among the converts."

"But I should think that in thirty years, if ever, Tavoy might have raised up native preachers that could look after things," said Katie.

"It had," Mrs. Bancroft answered. "Educated Tavoyans filled many a pulpit in Toungoo and Henthada. They had given their best as missionaries."

"They had better have looked after their own region first," said Charlie.

"Just as Massachusetts young men ought to stay in Massachusetts, instead of going out West and leaving the Bay State to foreigners. I agree with you," remarked Walter.

As Charlie had that forenoon vehemently expressed his determination never to settle in the East, and had held a sharp debate with Walter about it, the indorsement was unwelcome. "But these were converted heathen," he said: "that made it different."

"I've noticed that converted heathen are wonderfully like converted other folks," replied Walter.

"The preachers were needed where they went," said Mrs. Bancroft, "and could well have been spared from Tavoy, if the missionary force from abroad had been sustained. But in December, 1853, Mr. Thomas writes, 'In one of the late "Macedonians," mention is made of Mr. Thomas's parish; but, if I have a parish, I am at a loss to know where it is. Whether it lies up the Tavoy, and onward to the Ya River, one hundred miles north, or in Mata and the region adjoining, some seventy-five miles east; whether it be fifty miles south-east, in the Toungbyouk region, or in the Mergui province, extending to Kabin; or still farther up the Tenasserim River to a distance of one hundred and twenty miles from Tavoy,—I am unable to tell. But this is a fact: in all those places there are disciples and churches of Christ, and no missionary to guide them but myself.'

"No wonder that in many places piety waned,

prayer-meetings faded out, schools dwindled, and the craving for books that had marked the early converts gave place to the dull content of incipient starvation, or to the more easily gratified craving for strong drink."

"And the new missions were doing well all this time?" said Katie.

"Rather discouraging in regard to having any 'older missions.' Wouldn't it be well for the Missionary Union to imitate the early Hindoo mothers, and strangle or drown its children at the age of three years or earlier?" suggested Clarence.

"Not while they can show as good a record even as Tavoy in her darkest days. The Catholic priests came in, professing to be 'like the teachers, only better, because more lenient to the disciples' faults,' and tried their best to make proselytes, but soon found out that the Karens knew something of church history, and wearied of their fruitless work. The pastors were self-denying and earnest.

"'How much money have you?' asked Mr. Cross of a pastor who had just handed in his church's contribution of twenty-one rupees.

"'Fourteen rupees,' was the answer.

"'I will make it up to twenty-one,' said Mr. Cross. 'We can no longer give the four rupees a month which have come in past years from America, and there is no appropriation for a school in Tavoy this year.'

"The pastor took the money reluctantly, and walked away, looking sad, and, Mr. Cross thought, dissatisfied with the smallness of the sum.

"Two hours later the missionary was undeceived. The pastor came back, bringing six of the seven rupees, with the request that they be used 'to have a school in Tavoy.'

"Others showed a like spirit, and there were laymen scarcely less earnest.

"'Would to God that I had done as much as this man for Christ!' said Commissioner Haughton, as he saw at the Tavoy Association a feeble cripple, who had gone alone into a heathen neighborhood, gathered a school, and one by one led his neighbors to his Saviour.

"Many of the churches wholly sustained their pastors; and in 1862, hearing of the war and financial embarrassment in America, the Karens of Tavoy sent one hundred and ten rupees to the Missionary Union.

"When Mr. Colburn went there in 1864, he

found the orphan churches strict in discipline, and, though complaining much of coldness, as spiritual as most churches in America.

"From that time the Tavoy churches have been thrown almost entirely upon their own resources, scarcely ever having more than one missionary family, rarely the full services of one, and much of the time being left wholly alone. As a result, the number of church-members has decreased to eight hundred and sixty-five. At their earnest request, Mr. and Mrs. Morrow were sent to them in the autumn of 1876; and at present the Christians seem encouraged, and in several places there are marked signs of awakening among the heathen.

"Ten years had passed without a single conversion from heathenism among the Burmans of Maulmain. Only strangers came to the zayats. The missionaries met few in the streets to whom the gospel was news, and all others seemed hardened against it. Still the church of one hundred and thirty-eight held well on its way, supporting itself and a native evangelist besides, and gathering in converts from the school and the children of Christian families.

"Among the Karen churches of the district

there was rarely growth, sometimes loss. Contact with foreigners had given the Karens new ideas of the importance of money. There were speculators — English, Irish, German, Burman, and half-caste — ready to give them good wages as lumber-men. Those who accepted were obliged to work Sundays, expose themselves constantly to disease and accident, and trust to luck or their own wits for justice when the work was done. Of many a place it might be written, as Mr. Hibbard writes of Kyong, 'It has suffered severely from the lumbering mania: they have lost many hundred rupees, besides several souls and some bodies.' Among the oldest of the Karen churches, they were far less ready to support themselves than those of Toungoo and Henthada.

"When Mr. Bixby joined the Maulmain Burman mission, in 1853, he chose as his teacher Ko Boke, partly for his superior talent, partly that he might have a heathen constantly under his influence.

"At first, Ko Boke was wholly wedded to idolatry; but gradually the chains loosened.

"'This is a wise book,' he said one day as they read the Bible together: 'English books are full of wisdom.'

"'Not because it is an English book, but because it is God's book,' said Mr. Bixby.

"At another time, when Ko Boke seemed more than usually inclined to defend the religion of his fathers, Mr. Bixby took him to an idol-house.

"'I have come here,' he said, 'to preach to these gods,' and at once began an animated sermon.

"'Why, teacher!' interrupted Ko Boke: 'they cannot understand you.'

"'If they understand you when you pray to them,' said Mr. Bixby, 'they understand me when I preach to them.'

"Ko Boke appeared extremely mortified. 'They are nothing but earth and water,' he said: 'I will not worship them any more.'

"He afterwards told Mrs. Bixby that he was never in his life so ashamed as when the teacher took him to hear him preach to the gods.

"Weeks passed; and one day, after reading the fifty-fourth of Isaiah, he said, 'I can not and will not believe in Gaudama and Nigban. Formerly this religion was all dark to me: now it is a little light, and Gaudama's all dark.'

"One day in February, 1854, they started on

an excursion of twenty miles on the Gyne to Terraneh. About seven o'clock they found themselves fast on a sand-bank.

"'How shall we push off?' asked the missionary.

"The night was fearfully dark. 'The alligators are plenty, and several men have been killed here; let us wait till morning,' said the boatman.

"But Mr. Bixby dreaded the sun more than the darkness.

"'I am not afraid,' said Ko Oung Moo, the native assistant. 'The eternal God is here. He can shut the mouths of the alligators, as he did the mouths of the lions.'

"Jumping into the stream, he pushed off the boat, and they were soon on their way. Without knowing it, Ko Oung Moo had preached one of his best sermons.

"'May I preach at Terraneh?' asked Ko Boke presently as the boat glided smoothly on.

"'You may talk about Jesus all you can,' said Mrs. Bixby; 'but we want most that you should repent of your sins, and become a disciple.'

"'I am almost convinced; but it is very difficult.'

"But the next day he was a constant help in

interpreting and illustrating the arguments of the missionary, and the next he for the first time prayed audibly to the eternal God.

"Months passed, and Mr. Bixby could hardly doubt Ko Boke's conversion, but was greatly troubled by his dread of baptism.

"'I believe, and ought to be baptized,' he said; 'but I am ashamed to profess Christ.'

"Then his children and brothers would beg him not to forsake them.

"'Don't be so anxious about me, teacher,' he said at another time: 'God will give me strength to do this duty by and by.'

"'I fear your deceitful heart will mislead you; and, the longer you delay known duty, the more difficult it will be.'

"'But, teacher, you remember, that, before we went to the jungle, I was ashamed to go from house to house with you. I would not so much as sing a hymn with you; but now I love to go with you, and read and talk and sing about the true God and Jesus Christ. This is because God has given me great grace and strength; and will he not give me strength to endure baptism?'

"His words proved true. In October, 1855, he was baptized.

"'We have reason to rejoice and take courage,' said Ko Oung Mŏo, 'especially as he cannot see a man without desiring to preach to him.'

"From the schools, the jungle-trips of Mr. Bixby, and the brief tour of Mr. Brayton among the Pwos of the newly-conquered regions just north of Maulmain, might be gathered any number of incidents.

"'Where is your God?' asked a heathen father of his little son, a mission schoolboy.

"'Where is my father's god?' asked the boy.

"'There,' said the father, pointing to a pagoda and images.

"'Our God we cannot see; but he sees us: my father can see his god; but his god cannot see him,' replied the child.

"The home-thrust was too much for the father, and he chastised the child; but that did not prevent his continuing to attend the school and to pray to the 'unseen God.'

"'Are you Jesus Christ's man?' asked a listener in one of the jungle villages.

"'Yes.'

"'Well, I heard one of those men preach about ten years ago; and he told me many strange things, and gave me a very strange book; and since then I do not worship Gaudama any more.'

"'Ah! whom do you worship?'

"'The living God,' he answered, pointing upward. 'During these ten years I have been trying to find one of Jesus Christ's men, who could tell me more; but I could not find one.'

"There was a shade of sadness with the missionary's joy as he thought, 'This man may be but one of a thousand who are longing to find a Jesus Christ's man, and cannot.'

"'Come to my village,' urged the man, who proved to be a Peguan and a doctor. 'I have read the book to my neighbors, and some are pleased, and others displeased, with it. Come to my village.'

"The missionary promised.

"When, days afterward, the man caught sight of him coming up the river to fulfil the promise, he fairly danced for joy, exclaiming, 'Now we shall get the light; now we shall get the light!'

"And, until eleven at night, Mr. Bixby preached Christ to the listening company the old doctor had gathered together from his neighbors.

"Mr. Brayton, on his tour, entered a village where no white missionary had ever been seen; yet here was a band of four baptized by a native evangelist, and ten or fifteen others stigmatized by their neighbors as 'disciples of Christ.'

"In spite of Burman vigilance, some of them had learned to read. It was curious to hear them tell how they had secured their books from the enemy.

"'I put them in a chatty' (earthen box), said one, 'and tied them up in the top of a tree. The wind blew the chatty down, and smashed it: then I put them in a covered basket, and hid them in the jungle; but the rats gnawed a hole in the basket, and ruined many of the books: yet I have preserved from every foe a New Testament, hymn-book, and spelling-book.'

"No wonder they were overjoyed that a 'white foreign teacher,' with a fresh supply of books, had at last found them.

"After two years, Ko Boke was encouraged by the conversion of a doctor in the city. Other heathen grew more willing to listen. Baptisms became a little more frequent, and in 1869 we read of increasing interest in the city; while at Kimahwet, an outstation of Maulmain, four persons over fifty years old were baptized, five others were new converts, and many inquirers.

"The mission gained very slowly for the next

seven years. In 1876, after a missionary service of more than forty years, Dr. Haswell passed to the rest of heaven. In a few months his son, J. R. Haswell, followed him; but from the almost disorganized mission there comes a report of eighty-three baptisms, — a larger number than for many years before. At present the Burman Church numbers two hundred and seven, and those of the Karens nine hundred and thirty-eight.

"At all the stations, but especially at that Babel of all tongues, Rangoon, might often be found representatives of a race wholly unlike both Burmans and Karens, called Shans. Usually they had come for trading, or on pilgrimage to some holy place; for, like the Burmans and the Siamese, — the race to which they really belong, — they were Buddhists. Mrs. Ingalls mentions one time, when, on one of her tours with a native assistant, as he was trying to preach upon a foggy subject amid crying children and barking dogs, a hundred and fifty Shans came into the zayat, and immediately turned their corner of it into a cooking-place.

"At another time she speaks of meeting a company of them on a pilgrimage to the Rangoon pagoda.

"'Why have you come to the country?' they asked; and she told them.

"'Good,' was their answer. 'When shall you come into the Shan country?'

"Mrs. Ingalls had heard that question often, always with pain, and a silent prayer, 'God send some one to the Shans.'

"In December, 1860, Mr. Bixby, who had been four years in America, went out as their missionary. It is not often that the mountain comes to Mohammed: it did in this case, however, but not till Mohammed had started for the mountain. Mr. Bixby had but just reached Burmah, when he heard that a tribe of Shans, numbering several thousand, had taken refuge from oppressive Burman taxation in the British territory near Toungoo. Clearly Providence had brought his field half way to meet him: 1861 found him in it.

"The Shans listened to him respectfully, but timidly, doubting whether his coming really meant good to them. The idea of unselfish labor for others had never entered their minds, and they could not understand it. But the Burmans, who till then had had no missionary in Toungoo, showed unusual interest. Soon one, a woman, was baptized. Then came a re-action. For a while the name of Christ was heard only with a sneer; scoffers followed the missionary from place to place, ridiculing any who listened to him; tracts were rejected with insult.

"But one day, in the bazaar, Mr. Bixby was accosted by a young man with the always-welcome question, —

"'Are you Jesus Christ's man?'

"'Yes.'

"'I have been reading your books. Have you not a tract called "The Tree of Life"?'

"'Yes.'

"'Well, it says so and so,' giving briefly the substance of the tract. And then he asked for another book that would give him greater light. Mr. Bixby saw him often after that. He proved to be a man of fine talent, a good English scholar, and one holding a high position under government. For three years he had been a believer, but ashamed to have it known.

"One morning he came to Mr. Bixby, and asked for baptism.

"'My shame is all gone,' he said, 'and I am bold to speak for Christ. My sins are all forgiven through Christ, and my heart is light and happy.'

"The value of such a gift to the mission could

hardly be estimated. At once he gave forty rupees from his salary to aid the work of the mission. Soon he was actively engaged in telling the story of Christ. Four others followed: one was banished by his wife and friends; another was dragged upon the ground; another, a woman, was spit upon by the priest; and the Burman vocabulary was emptied of insulting words for use against them. But all stood.

"After about a year, the Shan chief gained enough faith in Mr. Bixby to bring his son, a young man of twenty-one, to him for education.

"'But do not make a Christian of him,' he stipulated.

"'God only can make Christians,' said Mr. Bixby. 'But it is my duty to teach; and, if I cannot do that, it is of no use to make him my pupil. I shall not force him to worship, nor baptize him if he does not ask it, or is not fit for it.'

"'Well,' said the chief, 'take him, and be a father to him.'

"Soon the young man showed a preference for the Bible above all other studies.

"One morning a few weeks later, in talking with Mr. Bixby, he said, 'Teacher, idols are not God; Gaudama is not God: the Eternal only is God. What must I do to worship him?'

"With trembling joy Mr. Bixby directed him; and a few weeks later he was baptized, the first Shan convert.

"Others came; one, Leingtaka, a doctor, the best educated Shan in the community, and a most stubborn Buddhist. For some time he had been Mr. Bixby's teacher. The superiority of Mr. Bixby's medicines, and of the spirit with which he gave them, first drew his attention. At last, after long conflict, he came for baptism. With him came a sprightly young Shan, his former priest.

"'I have given him rice and many offerings,' Leingtaka said playfully, 'and they have all gone to Nigban. We want to be baptized, and henceforth follow Christ.'

"Everywhere Leingtaka went, he told of Christ. Very soon he had gathered five converts in his own village.

"There was need of a zayat; and the deputy commissioner gave Mr. Bixby a plot of land, the site of a ruinous old pagoda. Such were plenty in the neighborhood, and no one thought of repairing them; but the priests were indignant.

"'There is a great amount of silver at the base of the pagoda,' they said.

"'Dig for it, and take it away, then; I do not want it,' replied the missionary.

"For several days they dug, but in vain.

"'We want to rebuild the pagoda,' was the next plea.

"Mr. Bixby knew this was false, and refused to yield.

"'It is an awful sin for you to build on so sacred a spot,' said the priests.

"Even some of the converts feared no one would go near the zayat, if built there. The excitement was intense. 'Go on with the building,' said Leingtaka, who knew the Poongyees better. Then turning to them, and pointing to the pagoda, he said, 'This little god has been so neglected, that the trees and grass have grown all over him; and they had become so heavy, that the god complained bitterly of weariness: so Teacher Bixby has had compassion upon him, and cut away the bushes. Furthermore, for a long time, you have not visited him; you have given him no rice, no offerings, but have given all your attention and offerings to the great Paya over yonder (pointing to a great pagoda on the hill): therefore this little god has become jealous of you, and has gone over to a better teacher.

You thought it would be a great sin for Teacher Bixby to build even by the side of this little god; but you could dig into his side and take out his bowels, and carry them off, in your greed for gold, and yet there would be no sin.' Then, becoming serious and earnest, he told them of the true God, closing an eloquent sermon with the words, 'Brethren, grass does not grow on God.'

"By the close of March, 1863, Mr. Bixby had a church of thirty warm-hearted brethren and sisters gathered about him, of whom nineteen were Shans. In the last days of the same year he started with Mrs. Bixby on a trip to Shanland.

"The home of the Shans lies between Burmah and Siam. It must be reached through unknown and hostile regions. Before Mr. Bixby started, the courage of most of his attendants failed; but he engaged others, — Shans, Burmans, Karens, and a Madras man, — and went on. Now up almost insurmountable hills, then through almost unfathomable mud, occasionally varying the scene by a tumble from their ponies, they entered the heart of the glorious mountain-region. No bird flitted over their heads; no squirrel ran across their path; no fly buzzed in the air. A mosquito would have been almost welcome in this utter lifelessness; but none came. Men there were, and the few animals man brings with him and plants abundantly; but nothing between.

"At last they reached a Geckho village. Thus far, no missionary had gone among the Geckhos; but they were well acquainted with each other by reputation. Before Mr. Bixby started on his journey, the intrepid Sau Quala had warned him, 'The Geckhos are cut-throats: do not go among them; they will kill you.'

"The impressions which the Geckhos had received of the missionaries were scarcely more favorable. As the party approached, women, children, and many of the men, fled. Others crept around in the thickets, armed with spears, poisoned arrows, and guns, which they levelled at Mr. Bixby's attendants. But at last Mr. Bixby partly re-assured them.

"'When men come to fight, they do not bring their wives along,' said the chief. 'Let them come up.'

"They were received by a semicircle of armed men, who retreated as they advanced. Once at the village, Mr. Bixby tried to talk with them.

"The chief was shy and sullen. 'An armed

force was sent here by the English Government,' he said. 'They destroyed our property, cut our men to death with dahs, seized and imprisoned our chiefs, and all for no offence whatever.'

"Anger flashed from all the other faces as the chief spoke.

"'But I am no government-officer,' said Mr. Bixby. 'I am a teacher of the religion of Christ.'

"The excitement grew stronger.

"'They were Christians that fought us,' they exclaimed, 'and they were sent by the Toungoo teachers.'

"'I will lay your case before government,' he said, 'and they will do right. Probably they did not know the facts of the case.'

"The chief's countenance changed. 'Then this teacher is our friend,' he said.

"'Yes,' answered the people: 'this teacher is our friend.'

"Next he proposed 'drinking truth' with Mr. Bixby. As 'drinking truth' is only the Geckho way of promising to keep, to a limited extent, the Golden Rule, and Mr. Bixby intended to keep it in any case, he agreed. A pig was killed, and its vitals cooked with pepper and salt for the covenant.

. "The people grew familiar, pulled open Mr. Bixby's bags, tried on his riding-cap, and peered into Mrs. Bixby's basket. At last they caught a glimpse of his revolver, and reached out eager hands for it.

"'No: you must not even look at it in this crowded house; but come down stairs with me, and you shall see how it is made.'

"Talking was useless. The crowd pressed upon him on all sides. Accidentally a cartridge was discharged, and the ball lodged in the breast of one of the young men. Preparations for drinking truth ceased instantly. Fierce, distrustful eyes glared upon Mr. Bixby. Plainly, if the wound proved fatal, more than one life would be lost. Mr. Bixby took the boy to his room, and nursed him more anxiously than if he had been his own.

"It proved to be only a flesh-wound. In the evening they 'drank truth,' though a few refused to unite in it; among them the brother of the young man.

"'If he lives,' he said, still clinging to his spear, 'it will be well.'

"On Sunday, Mr. Bixby preached to them; but every hour brought some fresh alarm. All night long, signal-fires were kept burning, 'that the women might see to catch rats for breakfast,' they said. Possibly, as he looked at them, Mr. Bixby had something of a fellow-feeling with the rats. By morning the wounded man was better, and the people made their morning-calls on the missionary *without guns.*

"Three days of rather monotonous travel brought the party to Shan-land. Perhaps it would have varied the monotony if they could have heard a conversation among the Shans and coolies on the second night. It was after this sort : —

"'The teachers have five hundred rupees in silver, and two hundred in gold. When we have crossed the border, and are in the jungle, it will be a good time to kill them and the assistants, burn the tent and bodies, take the money and provisions, and go where we please. No one will ever know what has become of them.'

"'Yes : then I could wear gold in my ears.'

"'I was leader of a band of banditti in this region. I know a hundred and fifty men of my sort in these mountains. If we fail, we can deliver them into their hands.'

"'But we shall not fail. If we are prevented

to-night, we can do it to-morrow. If any of the coolies refuse to join, they can be given up to the banditti, and killed.'

"Persuaded thus, the coolies all agreed to join. The leader pierced a vein in his arm, mingled the blood with kyong, and gave all to drink.

"'I,' he said, 'will put a spear through Mr. Bixby while he is asleep.'

"'And I,' said the one who wanted 'gold in his ears,' 'will kill Mrs. Bixby and the head assistant.'

"'The rest,' they added, 'will be afraid, and shiko to us; and we can kill them at leisure.'

"But the plot was too horrible for three of the coolies: before evening, they had betrayed it to Mr. Bixby. Then Mr. Bixby remembered that his Shan attendants had insisted on his buying an extra supply of arms 'to defend himself and Mrs. Bixby.' Cautiously he revealed the plot to his Burmans and Karens. Before nine, the fires of the coolies, usually kept burning all night, were put out.

"Mr. Bixby, not caring to have his movements watched while his enemies were wrapped in darkness, put out his own fires too.

"Soon they heard a crashing in the bushes.

"'A wild elephant is coming!—fire, teacher, fire!' cried the Shans.

"Mr. Bixby discharged one shot from his double-barrelled gun.

"'Fire again!'

"'No: if you want to keep the elephants away, kindle your fires.'

"They kindled them a little, but soon put them out again. Another wild elephant was heard. A Shan jumped up, and started toward Mr. Bixby.

"'Don't you come here,' said Mr. Bixby.

"'There's an elephant, teacher.'

"'Go back, or I shall fire upon you. If you are afraid of the elephant, kindle your fires.'

"The fires were again lighted. Every little while the leader arose, looked around, came a little toward Mr. Bixby's tent, went back, and thrust his spear impatiently into the ground. There was no sleep on either side that night.

"Morning came at last. Mr. Bixby revealed the plot to his Geckho guides.

"'We must go back immediately,' they said; and so said the Burmans. Only one, a Karen, agreed to go on, if the teachers did.

"To go on into a hostile country, with murderers only for attendants, was not to be thought of. To dismiss the murderers, and let them loose where they could rally their hundred and fifty friends, was not much better. To take them back with them was dangerous; for the murderers were the stronger party. The only hope was in dividing them.

"In the morning, Mr. Bixby armed his best assistants, took a gun, and told the coolies that he knew their plot.

"A deprecatory growl was the reply. They suspected as much.

"'Several have confessed,' Mr. Bixby added.

"'Who have confessed? who have told any thing?' they demanded.

"'I certainly shall not tell.'

"Then came a storm of vociferation, denials, and questions.

"'Be silent, at the peril of your lives,' commanded Mr. Bixby. 'It is useless to talk. I know all your plans. Some have joined you from fear: those I can forgive. If they will take up their baskets, and go quietly back to Toungoo, I shall make no more complaint against them. Others have plotted willingly, because their hearts are bad, and they want money: they must go another way.' He then called the names of all but three, telling them, if they had no heart in this plot, to show it by coming and giving him their spears.

"All but one came. 'I have fault, and am afraid,' he said; but Mr. Bixby thought best to take him with him.

"The other three were fearfully enraged. Keeping them at bay with his gun, Mr. Bixby demanded their spears and dahs. They refused to give them up. Bringing his gun in range, he ordered one of the men to go and take them. It was done; and with heavy hearts the missionaries turned their faces homeward."

"It strikes me it would be rather a peculiar picture for the magazine," remarked Charlie, — "the missionary standing, with a company of the 'poor heathen' around him, levelling his gun at them."

"I fear Mr. Bixby's face didn't wear the expression of the ox between the altar and plough, lowing out, 'Ready for either,' just then," said Walter; "but I've always thought I should like that ox better if he'd been drawn shaking his horns a little."

"I doubt if he ever came nearer to realizing the spirit of those words than at that moment," said Mrs. Bancroft; "and he *had* ploughed a furrow, though not permitted to sow the seed.

"When he returned, he found the wounded Geckho boy still doing well.

"'Why go to them? why not send teachers to us, who want to learn?' asked a Geckho chief.

"Mr. Bixby laid before government the case of the attacked Geckho village. A commission sent to examine found their complaint just. . A few years before, some Christian villages had been attacked by Geckhos. The Karen police corps — a body perhaps as 'Christian' as most similar organizations in this country — sent by the deputy commissioner to arrest the attacking chiefs had mistaken the aggressors, and visited the wrong village. One of the arrested chiefs died in jail: the other was discharged through the intercession of Dr. Mason. Now, the wounded feelings of the villagers were soothed by a present of five keezees, — Shan bells, worth several hundred rupees, and greatly prized by them; and very soon half a dozen Geckho villages were clamoring for teachers. A year later, the Geckho chief proposed buying two ponies; not a very marked advance toward religion, if he had been an American: but Geckho superstition forbade ponies; and the native preacher rejoiced more at this victory over it than at the fact that one of the ponies was to be for his own use. The way to Shan-land no longer lay through a hostile country.

"Converts multiplied among the other mountaineers. At one time (in 1864) Mr. Bixby had accepted for baptism a company of fifty-five, — Geckhos, Bghais, Saukoos, and Padongs.[1] A part of them came from villages clinging to the hills on either side of a deep gorge, where a mountain-stream had chiselled out a beautiful baptistery.

"'Meet me at the gorge on Sunday,' he said, 'and all can be baptized at the same time.'

"'No, no, no!' came the answer: 'that will not do. We cannot all be baptized in the same water.'

"'But how is that?' asked Mr. Bixby.

"Then came the story of feuds, that had separated their villages far more widely than did the gorge and the mountain-stream.

---

[1] The general name *Karen* is applied by the Burmans to these, in common with all mountain-tribes. There are, however, considerable differences between them.

"'What!' exclaimed Mr. Bixby, amused, but still trusting his wild brethren: 'are not your old hearts dead yet? Are you going to take them with you into the church? What have you to do with dead hearts? Why! were you not washed in the same blood? Are you not joined to one Spirit? Are you not going to the same heavenly home? Who will put up a partition between you there?'

"'Oh! never mind, never mind, teacher. We will be baptized in the same water.'

"'How are you? where are you at the date of this letter? I have been in prayer for you now,' wrote a friend to Mr. Bixby on the 22d of May. On the morning of that day, on the ringing of the gong, Mr. Bixby and the company of converts from his side the river, dressed in their best crimson silks, went down the steep mountain into the gorge. Nothing was visible of the party from the other side.

"A call from one of Mr. Bixby's party, an answering shout from across the stream, and then Mr. Bixby's whole company shouted together. The others responded; the mountains caught up the sound; the opposite mountains re-echoed it; and soon the two parties were in sight of each other. A joyful greeting followed: they joined with each other and the hills in a song of praise; and then the fifty-five happy converts were led down into 'the same water.'

"Two years later, at Shwanaughyee, among the villagers who had received him almost on their spear-points, Mr. Bixby married a sister of the chief to one of his preachers, and received her with two others for baptism. At the same time, in Kyah Maing, another of the villages he passed through on his Shan trip, he organized a church of seventeen.

"Two years later, with Mr. Cushing, Mrs. Bixby, and Miss Gage, he made another trip through the country. Then every village was open to welcome him. Heathenism and intemperance had fled from Kyah Maing. Thirteen were ready for baptism. At Shwanaughyee the chief laughed heartily as Mr. Bixby playfully alluded to his first reception there. A Christian chapel was building there now. He attended a covenant-meeting, and listened to their confessions. Their very sins marked the greatness of the change: one had, when thirsty, eaten a cucumber not his own; another, in his anxiety to reach his sick teacher, had travelled several miles on the sabbath: but all were penitent; and, after the meeting, six were received for baptism.

"But from that trip Mr. Bixby was carried to Toungoo, dangerously ill. In May, 1869, he left for America.

"In 1870 Mr. Cushing took up his residence in Toungoo. The Shans are always a trading people, and so not often stationary. Left to themselves for more than a year, the Shan Christians had become much scattered. In 1871 an intelligent young Shan was baptized, and at once placed in charge of the school. Mr. Kelley, a young man of great promise, went out the same year, but after only eleven months in the field, while on a tour in the Shan states, was drowned. Six hundred miles from Toungoo, outside of British Burmah, under the protection only of the Burman king, lies the city of Bahmo. In the fall of 1876, after careful inspection, Mr. Cushing became satisfied that this place was at present the true centre of the Shan mission; and removed there, where he still remains, the only white missionary in Upper Burmah."

CHAPTER XIII.

ASSAM. — BRAHMANISM AGAIN.

"IF one works in the same line week after week, and there isn't the least bit of change, but every thing stays exactly as it was, what then?" asked Katie.

"Give up, and try something else," said Charlie.

"Change your style of working," said Walter.

"Stop and think whether the work was worth doing at all," said Clarence, guessing more nearly than the others the real bearing of Katie's question.

All these answers were thrown in while grandpa Sears, to whom the question was really addressed, was preparing to give his.

"A sensible person must have stopped and thought before beginning the work," he said; "and if he has, and has taken what seemed to him the best way of working, and it seems so still, he had better go on. The world we live in didn't seem to amount to much for a good many thousand years after it was created; but God didn't give it up and try another."

"But I don't believe the world was useless all that time," said Katie. "It was a lesson-book for the angels, if nothing more."

"The birds and sea-monsters didn't know it," answered grandpa. "Perhaps you, too, may be serving as a lesson-book for somebody."

"The work of at least sixteen hundred years seems to have been pretty thoroughly rubbed out in the flood," said Clarence.

"No, young man," said grandpa earnestly (he always spoke earnestly when addressing Clarence): "the world after the flood was what it was because there had been a world before the flood. God *never* rubs out his work. You'll know that some time,— before it is too late, God grant. 'He fainteth not, neither is weary.'"

"But he *knows* how his work will turn out in the end," said Katie. "If we did, we could tell what to do."

"We do," said grandpa.

Katie's next question was asked only by a look.

"'*We know* that our labor is not in vain in the Lord,'" he answered. "Katie, if you've undertaken something worth doing, and have gone to work for it in the best way you knew, go ahead. All fruit doesn't ripen on the outside first. Some doesn't till it is just ready to drop. Perhaps yours is that sort."

Walter never dreamed that this conversation had to do with him. Ever since that one night, months before, Katie had watched anxiously for the fulfilment of the hopes then awakened. Even during these last busy weeks her thoughts and prayers had gone out for him more than for any or all of the many fields into which her labor had been called. If a library-book was selected, company invited, or a lecture attended, the uppermost thought was always, "Will it help, or hinder, Walter?" and all her words and actions were carefully guarded, that she might not hinder the work she dared not hope she could directly help. But in all that time he had spoken no word to encourage her. The appearance of anxious thought that marked the weeks that followed had passed away, and she feared no decision had been reached. True, his gentleness and helpfulness, his interest in missions, his readiness to defend religion, remained; but she began to fear, that, as Charlie said, this was "only to be on the opposite side from Clarence."

And the saddest thought of all was, that, had she been a consistent Christian from the first, she might by this time have been able to help him.

"I suspect mother has a story of discouraging labor for you to-night," said grandpa.

"It will answer your question better than I could, perhaps."

"It will show you how God has answered it, which is better," said Mrs. Bancroft.

"To-night let us leave Burmah and our Buddhist and Karen friends, and journey to the north-east till we find ourselves among our old acquaintances, the Brahmans, in a land bordering closely upon Bengal, where Carey first raised the missionary standard in 1793. We are in Assam, a country where almost every thing might be done, and nothing is. Its forests offer material for building any thing, from a basket to a temple; its ground holds out perpetual cards of invitation in the shape of petroleum, coal, cotton, grain, spices, tea, and the fruits of both torrid and temperate climates; there are *eri*-trees for silk-worms, and *bargach*-trees for India-rubber, and trees bearing varnish and gums, and dye-stuffs of many colors. No wonder the old Brahmans, when, centuries before, they brought their gods here, fancied that the country took its name from *Asama*, 'unrivalled.' But when, in 1836, Mr. Brown and Mr. Cutter came here, they found what Carey found when he first set foot in Bengal, — a people poor and ignorant, leaving all their thinking to be done by the priests; a priesthood busiest in reaching out long arms to rake in rupees and annas, and in inventing new falsehoods with which to repay the trust of the people; 'the whole country one vast Sodom;' above it all, the swarm of gods worshipped in costly temples by rites only less vile than their own histories; and around, and binding all, the terrible chain of caste.

"And the same slow work was to be done here that Carey did in his first years in Bengal, with only this difference, — that the missionaries had converted the East-India Company in those forty years, and its officers were their warmest friends. C. A. Bruce, an agent of the company, first suggested the mission; and Capt. Francis Jenkins aided it with money and advice as liberally as if he had been a member of the Board.

"It was not to the Assamese that the missionaries were first sent. Besides them, there were in Assam Ahoms, Khamtis, and other Shan races, all closely allied to each other, and members of the Siamese family; Bengalis, and the usual host of ruder tribes, Mikirs, Nagas, Kakhyens, Garos, Kosaris, — wandering races, — most plenty on the hills, kind to those they liked, cruel to those they disliked, but arranging their likes and dislikes upon principles so arbitrary, that no man's fate among them could be predicted beforehand. Over most of them the Brahman divinities held no sway. They believed vaguely and theoretically in a God, strongly and practically in devils or evil spirits, and charms. Besides this, each tribe held its own theory, or none, of prayer and sacrifice, and an after-death where there were boiling oceans, and fields of fire, and frail bridges over awful chasms, and beyond them thrones and pleasant fields, and happiness, or at least laziness, for the good.

"The first aim of the missionaries was the conversion of the Khamtis. Their first settlement was in Sadiya. Their first months were given principally to the study of the language and translations.

"In October, 1836, Mr. Thomas and Mr. Bronson, with their wives, sailed to join the mission. After they had crossed the ocean, and sailed for two months on the Brahmapootra, Mr. Bronson was taken sick. Mr. Thomas hastened on in a small boat to procure medicine. When within three hours' sail of Sadiya, two loose trees on the bank fell into the river, crushing the boat, and drowning Mr. Thomas almost instantly.

"Mr. Bronson removed in a few months to Jaipur, south-west of Sadiya, attracted chiefly by its situation in a desirable neighborhood."

"Of English officers?" asked Charlie.

"No. Mr. Bruce lived there; but the neighbors whose acquaintance Mr. Bronson especially sought were the Nagas, who made their home in the hills near by. They were one of the strongest of the hill-tribes, and are best described by their chief, from whom Mr. Bronson asked leave to teach them.

"'The Nagas,' said he, 'are like birds and monkeys, lighting on this mountain, and stopping on that; and no white man can live among them to teach them. As soon as the boys are old enough, they put into their hands the hatchet and spear, and teach them to fight and make salt. Beyond that they know nothing.'

"Mr. Bronson did not enter their village wholly without a welcome. A cook-house was at once built for him, a spring of water given up to his company, and eggs, milk, and potatoes brought and set before them; but, immediately after, a long council was held concerning him (followed in due time by six others). He read the Ten Commandments to them. Some they heard with a sneer; but others, especially the second and eighth, they approved; for, though they worshipped evil spirits, they were no idolaters, and stealing was a capital offence among them. Once Mr. Bronson attended one of their funeral ceremonies.

"'What divinity has taken away our friend? Who are you? Where do you live?—in heaven, or on the earth, or under the earth? Who are you? Show yourself. If we had known of your coming, we would have speared you,' sang the chorister.

"'Yes,' responded the people, brandishing their dahs.

"'We would have cut you in pieces, and eaten your flesh.'

"'Yes,' responded the people, waving their glittering spears in defiance.

"And these questions and threats might almost be said to comprise the sum of Naga theology.

"An armed attack upon Sadiya by the Khamtis, whom they had come to convert, was one of several arguments which led the missionaries to remove to Jaipur. The military followed; then the inhabitants; and Sadiya was 'abandoned to tigers and jackals.'

"Mr. Bronson was visiting his neighbors in the Naga hills at the time of the attack. He hastened to Jaipur, fearing for his family, who were there; but the place was not attacked. Here, in May, 1840, he met his sister (Miss Rhoda Bronson) and Mr. and Mrs. Barker. His sister went with him at once to the Naga hills, where he had moved his family. Mr. and Mrs. Barker remained about a year at Jaipur, and then moved to Sibsagor. Mr. and Mrs. Brown soon followed.

"Miss Bronson's work was finished almost before it was begun. Constant fever obliged her and her brother to leave the hills. In December, 1840, she died at Jaipur. In October, 1841, Mr. Bronson moved to Nowgong. Chiefs and people had learned to love him.

"Translation was Mr. Brown's principal work; printing, Mr. Cutter's. In addition, Mr. Brown preached at Sibsagor and the surrounding villages, and found time for frequent less regular encounters with the Brahman gods. Sometimes, taking a prism for a text, he would prove that the rainbow was not Vishnu's bow, with which the god shot the demons who were trying to drink the rain; or, with a triangle roughly marked on a board, he showed that the height of trees and buildings could be told without climbing them; and how the moon's distance had been measured, and found not to be sixteen hundred thousand miles; and that the sun was almost four hundred times, instead of only half, as far off as the moon. He told them he had come from a land beneath their feet, and seen that there was no Mount Meru eighty thousand miles thick, nor room for one; nor for the five elephants on whose heads, each eight thousand miles thick, the earth stood; nor for the four oceans of rum and milk and butter and sugar: and yet all these things were in their Shasters. And the people listened, wondered, then perhaps turned to the priests with the question, 'What have you to say?' And the priests were sometimes silent, sometimes angry; but neither priests nor people could help *seeing*. Discussions among themselves grew common.

And there were other signs that showed very slowly, but really, in the little circle around the stations, that Brahmanism was fading out; but as yet, after five years of labor, there was not one sign that Christianity would take the place left vacant.

"'I cannot alter my religion,' said one of the best informed. 'It would subject me to want; for, being a Brahman, I cannot work.'

"Probably he spoke what many thought; and the lower castes followed the Brahmans.

"One day in May, 1841, just before Mr. Brown left for Sibsagor, there came to him Nidhiram, one of the apprentices in the printing-office, asking the longed-for question, 'What shall I do to be saved?' It had been asked before, but only as a man at home, and meaning to stay there, might idly ask the nearest route to China. This man was in earnest. The next day he came again. Again Mr. Brown pointed him to Christ.

"'I *am* willing to give myself into the hands of God,' he said at last.

"In the afternoon he came, rejoicing in God. Two weeks later he was baptized. He dropped the name of the heathen god Ram, and took, instead, that of Levi Farwell.

"Six months later another was baptized, awakened by reading a tract, 'The True Refuge.' In June, 1842, at Sibsagor, two others were awakened,— Semai and Kolibar. Both left off opium, and came regularly to pray with the missionaries. But old habits were too strong. Soon Kolibar went back to his opium. The next step was to send word to the missionaries that he would pray at his own house, instead of theirs; and for a long time little was heard from him.

"In the autumn of 1843 Mr. Cutter removed with his press to Sibsagor.

"In February, 1845, the head printer, Batiram, was taken sick, and sent for Mr. Cutter.

"'Can none of the Hindoo gods whom you have worshipped save you?' asked Mr. Cutter.

"'Oh, no! my mind is not in the least inclined to think of them,' was the answer.

"'Do you think Jesus Christ can pardon your sins?'

"'Oh, yes! and I have believed this truth for the past two years, and I have prayed to him night and morning for nearly that time, without the knowledge of a single human being, except the lad who lives with me.'

"The next day he was better. 'Will you not

pray with me?' he asked as Mr. Cutter arose to leave.

"'For what shall I pray?' asked Mr. Cutter.

"'That I may obtain a new heart, and have my sins pardoned,' was the answer.

"Every day brought new evidence that Batiram was converted. On the 24th he surprised Mr. Cutter by asking to have all the men in the office called together, that he might read and pray with them.

"There, before them all, he confessed his faith in Christ, and his cowardice in not owning him earlier. Two weeks later he was baptized. He stood bravely a storm of ridicule from his relatives; and in a few months his cousin, Ram Sing, one of the bitterest of his opposers, joined him as a Christian. A little earlier the old inquirer Kolibar had forsaken his opium, and joined the church. Soon Nidhi Levi and Batiram were engaged with Mr. Brown in preparing an Assamese hymn-book.

"In 1846 the annual missionary meeting was held at Nowgong. Before it closed, seven from the orphan institution were baptized. Others not connected with the institution were converted. The same year five were baptized at Sibsagor, and two by Mr. Barker at Gowahati.

"In January, 1850, Mr. Barker died on his way to America. A month later his place was filled by Mr. Däuble, a German Lutheran missionary in Assam, who for years had had doubts on the subject of baptism, but repressed them because of the contempt in which Baptists were held in his own country. Coming to Assam, acquaintance with the missionaries altered his views of their denomination; and he commenced earnest investigation. On the 24th of February he was baptized. Three intensely earnest years, spent in the school, the street, and the jungle, finished his work. He died March 23, 1853.

"In November, 1847, Messrs. Danforth and Stoddard, and in July, 1850, Messrs. Whiting and Ward, with their wives, left America for Assam.

"Except an occasional visit from cholera, small-pox, or a brother-missionary, for years life went on monotonously enough at the three mission stations. 'It is the trenches that try soldiers, not the battle,' is a saying just half true, but as true in the Christian warfare as in any. The main work in Assam was digging and pounding, undermining and battering walls that seemed immovable. If an opening at any time was made in one wall, it was only to reveal another wall behind it.

"'You must think me a great fool, if you suppose I would give up the merit gained by seventy years' service of Ram for the little I could gain by two or three years' service of Christ,' said an old man to Mr. Whiting. With the more thoughtless this was the most common objection. Convince them of the worthlessness of their 'merit,' and the next question would be, 'But, if I become a Christian, shall I not lose caste?' and at the answer, 'Yes,' many a hopeful inquirer turned away decidedly and forever. If deep conviction overthrew this wall, it was only to find a stronger one in the almost universal habit of opium-eating.

"All owned their sinfulness. 'Light sins' theirs were usually, — lying, stealing, and the like. They had never killed a cow, nor struck a Brahman: still they owned that such sins as they committed every day entitled them to almost infinite punishment. But then there was another side. The repetition, or even the hearing, of the name of a god, brought almost infinite merit: so the day would be given to vice or dishonesty; and at night, mumbling rapidly the name of Krishna or Ram, they would sink into the deep sleep of the opium-eater, feeling that their account was probably somewhere near square; or if not, and there was a balance of a million years or so on the wrong side, they could not alter what fate decreed.

"'You want to teach the people about Jesus Christ; but no one will listen to you, or receive your words,' was almost the first salutation Mr. Danforth met on entering one of their villages.

"'Ninety-nine out of a hundred will reject the gospel at first,' he answered; 'but in the end it will triumph. The reason so many reject it is they do not examine it. I am like a man coming among you bringing a hundred rupees in a box, and offering it to whoever will take it. Nine out of ten refuse to take the trouble. The tenth says to himself, "Why, it is no great trouble to open it; and there *may* be something in it." He reaches out for the box, opens it, and, lo! he is the possessor of a thousand rupees.'

"They saw the application, and seemed ashamed of their objection. They listened with surprise as he told them of the triumphs of Christ in Burmah and Bengal, and of the converts in Assam. A gurn and two Brahmans came up, and the people dispersed.

"But as he went through the village, and beyond it, their first words seemed to him almost like a prophecy.

"The only thing that always arrested attention was the relation of Christian experience. Those who are ignorant of both can match Shaster against Bible, Krishna against Christ, as well in Assam as in America; and the Assamese knew scarcely any thing of their own scriptures. But for Christ in the soul they had no parallel. Hindooism has no religious experiences, and they knew it. Often as Mr. Ward touched this theme, he was interrupted by the question, 'Can *I* obtain this inward witness? Tell us how we can obtain it.'

"In the beginning of the next year, two of the oldest girls in Mrs. Brown's boarding-school at Sibsagor were awakened and converted. Their joy aroused the four next younger, and for a while there was little study in the school; for Mrs. Brown found, if she left them, they would separate, each to find some room where she might pray alone.

"The next year brought more fruit; among it a Brahman girl and her mother. Ten years later there was a revival at Sibsagor, in which ten were converted, several from the school; and, before Mrs. Brown died, she had the joy of knowing that *all* who had been under her care in the school had become Christians. There were like scenes in the orphan institution at Nowgong, under Mr. Bronson's care, and in 1853 a revival in Mrs. Danforth's boarding-school at Gowahati.

"For some years Nidhi Levi and Batiram were active, earnest preachers. One day in January, in the midst of a tour with Mr. Whiting, as they were talking of their delightful work, Batiram said, 'Something whispers to me, "The time is short."' Four months later he met the last enemy as fearlessly and joyously as he had met all others. His mother, a strong-minded, sensible woman, had come with him to Sibsagor about a year before. A rigid Hindoo, Christianity seemed to her some dreadful infection. She loved her son as she would if he had taken the small-pox, and shrank quite as much from eating or living with him. A little shelter was built for her, and there she cooked and ate her solitary meals. But, when she saw her son carried through death as she had never seen human being carried through it before, she believed in the God he worshipped, and was angry with him,—angry that he had taken away the staff of her old age. For weeks she remained inconsolable.

"At last, one day she came to Mrs. Brown a picture of distress, and told her grief.

"'Do you ever pray?' asked Mrs. Brown.

"'Pray! What is there for me to pray for? I get nothing but trouble here. The Lord has taken away my son; and, if I pray at all, it is that he would take me too.'

"But from that time she began to attend prayer-meetings.

"At last, in a female prayer-meeting, she knelt and prayed, 'The Lord has taken away my dear son as a punishment for my sins. The will of the Lord be done. Have mercy upon me, a poor sinner, and fit me to join him in heaven. Have mercy upon my step-son and two daughters, who are in total darkness, and bring them to the light of this true religion.' Tears choked her, and she could go no farther. There was not a dry eye in the room. It was the turning-point; but more than a year passed before she *wholly* gave up caste and the charms she used for her ailments. This delayed her baptism.

But when, at last, she had forsaken all, and, after a few months, was told that she might now be baptized, she wept for joy.

"In 1853 Mr. Cutter's connection with the society closed; and Mr. Brown added printing to translating and preaching till 1855, when he left to repair in America the wear of more than twenty years' uninterrupted service. He had now, besides translating the catechism and part of Genesis into Shan, translated, and three times revised, the New Testament in Assamese, and translated most of Genesis, and the striking portions of other books of the Old Testament. These last were published as tracts, or in 'The Orunodoi,' a weekly Assamese newspaper started by the missionaries in 1846.

"Dark times followed. Opium-eating and intemperance increased fearfully with the English trade. Often, as the missionary passed from village to village, the hopeful inquirer of the year before would meet him with the stupid stare that told always the same story of slow poisoning for mind and body. Tea-planting brought to Assam large numbers of the most dissolute English, who enjoyed enticing converts into their employ. Yet by the heathen all white men were taken as types of Christianity. A few of the converts grew steadily stronger till death; more were at one time or another suspended or excluded; but most of the entire number were what Mrs. Bronson calls 'anxious comforts;' not wolves certainly, hardly sheep, but very puny lambs, needing constant nursing.

"For the first years the converts, driven from their former occupations by loss of caste, were taken into the employ of, or placed on land belonging to, the mission; and when Mr. Whiting found it necessary to break up this arrangement, and throw them upon their own resources, he says, 'I have been called by some of our native Christians such names as the Assamese vocabulary abounds with, and which, if expressed in English, would not be thought promotive of edification.'

"Then came the terrible years of 1857 and 1858, when the streets of Cawnpore and Delhi ran blood, and the missionaries in Assam expected daily to share the fate of their brethren in Hindostan. For six months, Mr. Danforth drilled daily, in soldier garb, in full view of a large company of mutinous Sepoys, that he might be prepared to defend his family and the mission property to the last. Then sickness drove one after another from the field, till, for a year, Mr. Whiting was the only missionary in Assam. Mr. Tolman came in 1859: but almost from the first his health failed; and, in less than two years, he returned to America; not, however, till he had welcomed Mr. Bronson and Mr. Ward back to Assam.

"In February, 1861, just before leaving for America, Mr. Whiting baptized three at Sibsagor, — the first for six years. The next month, six more were baptized by Mr. Ward; and the revival continued nearly through the year. Mr. Bronson took charge at Nowgong. The little interest rallied, and soon six converts were baptized there.

"Among the first acquaintances the founders of the Assam mission made were the Mikirs, less savage than many other hill-tribes, generally drunkards, about one-tenth part opium-eaters.

"Their creed was simple, — 'God will reward those who do right, and punish those who do wrong.'

"'What is it to do wrong?' asked the missionary.

"'Not to worship God, to steal, and to cut each other in pieces, is wrong: the opposite is right.'

"Mr. Tolman made a long tour among them in 1859, talked with them in 'broken Assamese seasoned with Mikir,' and received for answer, 'Your words are good and true; but, if we should receive them, the mountain-spirit would kill us at once.'

"But fever, the '*real* mountain spirit,' made the missionary its prey almost before his work was begun; and early in 1861 he was obliged to leave the country, not to return.

"Still the Mikirs came often to the mission-house at Nowgong; and some learned to read.

"'Monkeys!' said the Assamese. 'You have no religion of your own, and so come to the Padre Sahibs to learn one.'

"In December, 1862, Mr. and Mrs. Scott arrived as their missionaries.

"'The Tolman white teacher attempted to live among the hills, and teach the new religion, but was quickly driven away by the deities: so the same angry deities will send fever among the new teachers if they attempt to visit them; and among the people will be a curse,—failure of crops, and sickness,' predicted the Mikir prophets.

"Already the commissioner, Major Hartson, had promised a monthly donation of fifty rupees for a normal school among them; and Rong Bong, a Mikir chief, had started a new village, and built a house and schoolhouse for the teacher he believed would some time come. Mr. Scott made a tour among his parishioners, and then started a Mikir school at Nowgong, which soon grew to twenty-five, most of them intelligent, active young men, whose time was valuable at home.

"'Here is my son, whom his father and mother love very much,' said a Mikir chief as he brought Mr. Scott his little boy. 'Our people are all ignorant, and we who are old must die so; but the children may learn wisdom. With his mother's consent, I have brought our son to give him to you. We wish him to become a Christian, and a wise and good man. Take him, and be a father to him.' And, without waiting for a reply, the chief turned away; while the missionary prayed, 'Lord, give me such confidence in thee.'

"A field was kept where they could work for

their support. They were generally willing, active laborers; but at one time Mr. Scott was obliged to call to account three or four of them for tardiness. Their hung their heads in silence, and he was about to reprove them.

"'Yes,' said one bolder than the rest, 'it is our fault. We are ashamed; but last night, as we sat down to read God's word, and pray together, before going to sleep, we found so many good words, that we kept on reading and talking about them till the morning light came. Then we lay down, and overslept our time.'

"On inquiry, he found that they often so spent half the night.

"In the last days of 1864 Mr. and Mrs. Scott made an interesting visit to the Mikir hills. But the words of their prophets were fulfilled to the letter, and through 1865 missionary work was done mainly in the sick-room. But this seemed most effective of all. Several were converted. One was impatient to carry the news to his native hills.

"'But the streams are swollen, and the poison miasma fills the jungle,' said Mr. Scott.

"'I know it well,' was the answer; 'but what are such miasmas compared with the pains of a lost soul? If I delay till the jungle is safe, my father, brother, and sister may all die without a Saviour.'

"In 1866 Mr. and Mrs. Scott left for America. The fulfilment of the predictions of their prophets led to the withdrawal of a number of Mikir youth from the school. Two prominent converts, one the old Mikir chief Rong Bong, fell away; and such efforts were made to seduce the rest, that Mr. Scott, on his return in 1868, pronounced 'each day of faithful living, by one of these poor, weak disciples, scarcely less a miracle of grace than the first awakening to new life.'

"The same year came one of the terrible cholera seasons common in the East. Mr. Scott labored incessantly among the sick and dying for six months, and then himself fell a victim. Mrs. Scott was at once invited to Sibsagor; but she could not leave her Mikirs. 'I gave myself to the work of missions before ever I knew my precious husband,' she said; and alone, with the care of three children, she took charge of the station.

"And at last, at the close of 1869, the Mikir mission was able to report 'a year of steady progress.' The work in the hills was well carried on by Habe and Mon, two former pupils; several were converted in the school; wanderers returned; while there seemed to be a gradual waking-up among those outside.

"'Yes, yes,' said old Rong Bong, 'I see it all. I see how those young men are leading our people out of the wilderness; and I, alas! who should have been an Omed, am an outcast from God, reaping the bitter fruit of my sins.'"

"Who was Omed? and what had he done?" asked Edith.

"To answer that question, I must tell you the story of Gowahati and the Garo mission, and give you the record of the most successful series of failures in our missionary history.

"In 1843 Mr. Bronson started an orphan institution at Nowgong. At first it promised to be a true nursery for the church. Certainly children brought under the eye, and almost into the family, of the missionary, with caste already broken, — its wall separating them from heathenism, instead of from Christianity, — could be 'educated into Christian character,' if anybody could. But the test of years proved that the separation often made temptation more dangerous when it came; that to find honorable employment for the orphans as they grew up was not easy; that with small-pox, fever, cholera, impatience, indolence, and total depravity, among the pupils, the care of the institution demanded the whole time of one missionary; and often there was but one at Nowgong. The heathen, instead of being impressed by such an example of Christian benevolence, said, ' You will break our caste, unfit us to enter any one's house, and then cast us off to starve;' a false charge, but not without effect. In 1856 the orphan institution was given up. Two years later, but five Christians could be found in Nowgong.

"True, some promising ones had moved away, and some had gone, happy and thankful, from the asylum to a home in heaven. But promising ones do not always perform, when scattered, one in a place, among heathen neighborhoods; and the dead do not increase the annual tables of statistics, — to some eyes the ultimate object of all missions.

"Perhaps, if it could *then* have been known that from the dispersed orphans 'more Christian helpers would be raised up than from any other one instrumentality,' the sending of an additional missionary might have seemed a better solution of the problem than the abandonment of the enterprise; but this was hidden in the future.

"In 1844 Mr. Barker moved to Gowahati. Years passed by; conversions were few; missionaries died, or left disabled. Dishonesty, intemperance, opium-eating, and other vices, among the professed converts, and the certainty that at least half of the few inquirers came from no good motives, disheartened the always over-worked laborers. They made earnest, tearful appeals; but the chief ground of these appeals was the amount of seed already sown there, the mass of unmoved heathenism around, and the graves of missionaries. In fact, for years, the mission sustained to the Baptist denomination the relation of an unnecessary cat in a tender-hearted family,—tolerated, because nobody has the heart to kill it. In 1859 there was left there only a pastorless and almost invisible church, a tiny flock of half-grown lambs, so feeble, that the breath of life in them seemed hardly worth preserving, with only wolves to care for them, and the nearest shepherd a hundred miles away.

"Mr. Bronson made them a flying visit now and then from Nowgong, and wrote earnest letters home, begging, entreating, threatening almost, at times, till the people were tired of reading them; and 'The Macedonian' only noticed the receipt of 'one of Mr. Bronson's usual appeals for Assam.'

"So Gowahati was counted a failure.

"In 1856, Mr. Bion, an English Baptist missionary in Dacca, made a tour to Assam, touched at Gowalpara, preached, scattered tracts and books, and returned, reporting 'a wide door open for effort.' Nobody entered at the door: the tracts and books, so far as heard from, were torn in pieces, swept into the mud, or sold to others for a pice or two each.

"Mr. Bion's Assam trip was a failure.

"Among the mountains of Assam, for centuries past, have lived, fought, and died the Garos, — a race more savage and bloodthirsty, and far more truthful and honest, than any of the tribes around. For more than fifty years they had been a perplexing problem to their English neighbors. They were no cowards: their frequent raids upon the Bengalis at the foot of their hills proved that. Indeed, a Bengali skull was considered a necessary part of the furniture of a stylish Garo. Not many other things were necessary. A strip of cloth, with the addition of a dozen heavy ear-rings for the ladies, served for dress. For food they liked meat and ardent spirits. At great entertainments, these, too, must be served in a fresh human skull. On such occasions a puppy is coaxed to eat all the rice it will, and then thrown alive into the fire, and roasted, making a most *recherché* dish, — not at all more disgusting to us than our habit of drinking milk is to them.

"They have little in common with civilized races, except, perhaps, slavery, cotton-planting, and woman's rights: for among the Garos, while either party can propose marriage to the other, only the woman has liberty to reject a proposal; and, though man can divorce his wife only by giving up to her his children and all his property, a woman can divorce her husband at any time. In agriculture they are in advance of most mountain-tribes.

"They have no temples nor images, but worship by sacrificing white cocks, pigs, goats, bullocks, young, dogs, liquor, rice, and flowers to the spirits of these hills. Many a rich Garo has made himself poor by his fruitless efforts to persuade these deities or demons to keep their hands off.

"Such were the Garos in 1782, when Mr. Elliot was sent to 'inquire into the disturbances' among them; and such essentially were they in 1860, when they made their last great raid upon their Bengali neighbors.

"Under the eye of the British Government for a century, entirely surrounded by British territory for quarter of a century, they were still, according to the lieutenant-governor of Bengal, 'the most desperate and incorrigible tribe in all the British dominions.'

"Judging it by the same test we apply to missions, — the change wrought for the better, — the British conquest of the Garo hills was a failure.

"In 1849 Mr. Stoddard baptized Kandura, a boy of twelve years, from the orphan institution at Nowgong, then under his charge. The missionaries had already learned that giving the names of Judson, Boardman, and Carey to their orphans, was much easier than imparting characters to correspond. Perhaps it was on that account that to young Kandura was given the surname 'Smith,' which it might reasonably be hoped he would succeed in living up to. He proved to be a good scholar and business-man, and in time was appointed to an office under government, with a salary of forty rupees per month, at Gowahati.

"'Gowahati *must* have a pastor,' he said; and he spared neither pains nor money to obtain one; but all his efforts failed.

"Already he had charge of all the business-affairs of the church. At last he resigned his office under government, and, with a salary of fifteen rupees per month, took the pastorate of the Gowahati church.

"'Can you hold on till some one arrives?' asked Mr. Bronson.

"'My wish is to hold on *till death*,' was the answer.

"When Mr. Bion visited Gowalpara, there were at the government school there ten Garos. Some of them had learned to read Bengali. One of them, Omed, bought for 'a pice or two' one of the tracts Mr. Bion had distributed, and the Psalms of David. After a while Omed enlisted as a sepoy, and was placed on guard before one of the mission bungalows that had been rented to a British officer. In cleaning the house, some leaves of tracts were swept out. One of them, 'Error Refuted,' he picked up, and read. The conviction seized him that this was truth. He went to the native Christians for more books. His comrades became alarmed.

"'Omed,' they said, 'what is this you are doing? Are you going to become a *Kistan?*' (a word of cutting contempt.)

"Still he persevered. He gave his books and tracts to two others, Ramke and Rangku; and they, too, were awakened. Finally, he and Ramke were both baptized by Mr. Bronson into the church at Gowahati.

"'Is there no missionary for *my* people?' was Omed's first question; but there was none.

"'If there was a missionary here, or at Gowalpara,' they said, 'we would strike our names from the list of sepoys, and go teach our people; but we have no one to teach us, and we are too ignorant now to go forth. We often get worldly and wicked during the week; but when we come on the sabbath, and hear brother Kandura explain the Bible, our hearts get happy and fixed.'

"Both of them had good government situations; but at last, after remaining a year or more under Kandura's instruction, they resigned, and went out as missionaries.

"'I am sorry Omed wishes to leave the regiment, wrote his colonel, 'as he is a very steady, well-conducted sepoy; quite an example to many in the regiment.'

"'I am glad to see any one who is willing to attempt the reformation of those blood-thirsty savages; I hope you will succeed,' said the lieutenant-governor of Bengal to one of the missionaries, in a tone indicating the profoundest incredulity.

"In 1866 the third Garo, Rangku, was baptized. At the same time, there came, from eight Garos awakened by the preaching of Omed and Ramke, an appeal for help. Success awakened bitterest opposition. Thinking the tigers of the jungle safer neighbors than the human tigers of the hills, Omed removed to the valley, built there a grass hut, and lived there alone with his brave wife for a year, preaching to the Garos that passed on their way to market, and making visits to his old neighbors of the hills. Other families joined him. Finally a village was built there, — Rajamala, a city of refuge for persecuted Christians. As no missionary had visited them, of course none were baptized.

"In 1867 Mr. Bronson paid them a visit. At

Damra, Ramke had a school and public worship. Till a late hour they talked, and sang Christian hymns; and then all together knelt in prayer.

"At Omed's village a crowd waited to receive them. The village was clean; its forty houses new and orderly; and the largest and best was the place of worship, built wholly by the worshippers. Mr. Bronson carried with him a tent, but never pitched it; for a clean house was at once assigned him. He went to the chapel. It was crowded with eager listeners. He spoke in Assamese, and the assistants interpreted. They listened with intensest interest; but it was plain that Omed had already made the story of the cross familiar.

"At last Mr. Bronson asked, 'How many of you love this Saviour, and, abandoning all heathen practices, worship him alone?'

"Twenty-six arose.

"He charged them to examine their motives, and reminded them that their decision meant ridicule, reproach, opposition, perhaps death.

"'Yes,' was the answer: 'we have thought it all over. We expect opposition. We have decided.'

"The three native assistants — Rangku was

one of them — now testified to their changed conduct, and especially their abandonment of all heathen rites and intoxicating drinks. The last had cost some of them a severe struggle.

"All were accepted for baptism after careful examination.

"'I am Christ's disciple,' said a mountain Garo, one of the first to leave off opposition and join Omed, and his right-hand man ever since; 'but I cannot walk. How can I be baptized?'

"For three months he had been disabled by a diseased foot.

"'He can be brought to me in the water,' said Mr. Bronson, seeing his eagerness.

"When told this, his delight was plainly visible.

"'My heart burns with desire to tell my people on the mountains this religion,' he said. 'Only let my foot get well, and I shall go.'

"The next Sunday they were baptized, and, the same evening, organized into a church.

"'And now,' said Mr. Bronson, 'whom of the three assistants will you choose as your pastor, to baptize, bury your dead, and perform your marriages?'

"Unanimously they chose Omed; and then

and there Mr. Bronson ordained him, charging him to 'range the hills, preach, baptize, do the work of a Christian pastor, and be faithful unto death.'

"On Thursday, as he was leaving for Damra, Omed told him that ten others wished baptism. One of them was weeping.

"'You know that when my life was threatened for cutting bamboos on the mountain where the heathen sacrifice, and I had to flee to save it, I did not turn back,' he said to the native assistants.

"The church was called together, and the ten were received; Omed and Mr. Bronson baptizing alternately.

"Early in 1867 Kandura welcomed Mr. Stoddard and Mr. Comfort to Gowahati. Mr. Stoddard had been absent ten years. He went at once to the Garos, making Gowalpara his headquarters.

"When Mr. Stoddard arrived, it was too early to go among the hills; but his people came to him. So, very soon, he had the privilege of attending a Garo prayer-meeting.

"'O God,' prayed an old, blind, lame man, 'just like a decayed, rotten thing, so am I before thee! Save, Lord, or I perish.'

"'Brothers,' says a young Christian, 'pray for my parents. It is not two weeks since they decided to be Christ's disciples. I am very glad. How they opposed me a few weeks ago! Now the whole village is angry with them, and threatens to stone them from the place if they do not go back to devil-worship.'

"Chejing then prays: 'Pity me, O Lord! If you don't save, no one can. I have one leg in hell now.' He is not a Christian, but wishes to be.

"Another speaks in Garo. He has been a bitter opposer, and this is his first confession: 'I have stopped my fight, and all the devil-worship with it. I will now serve and obey Christ.'

"Before Mr. Stoddard can strike a tune, Rudram is on his feet: 'I have nòt been baptized; but I love Christ. I am a Christian at all hazards. My parents are among tigers because they have recently professed Christ.'

"And the best of it is, that the missionaries know all this is sincere; for the word, even of heathen Garos, can be trusted.

"On his first tour, as, with Mr. Ward, Mr. Stoddard entered Omed's village, he found young and old, male and female, drawn up as if in military array to receive them.

"'This is the Lord's army,' said Mr. Ward.

"Omed repeated the words.

"'Yes, we are the Lord's sepoys,' came the response from all along the line.

"Mr. Ward preached in Assamese, Omed and Ramke interpreting by turns. Once, as a line of thought was touched on which he felt deeply, Omed, forgetting the missionary, and every thing else but the matter in hand, spoke on rapidly, and with intense earnestness, for half an hour. Mr. Ward looked at his brother-missionary, and smiled, quite willing to sit down. It was clear, from the absorbed attention of all, that Omed was striking the right spot.

"There was no consciousness of official dignity about Omed. He was a gentle, sedate man of thirty-five, heartily loved and revered by his people.

"Mr. Stoddard's journal for the next year, during which he became acquainted with his field, is the record of a succession of 'joyful surprises.' The steadfastness of the disciples under trial, their missionary zeal, the frankness of the inquirers, the springing up of new interests, were a perpetual delight to him.

"But even he could not feel the peculiar joy

that filled Kandura's heart, as a little later, with Mr. Comfort, he travelled and preached through this region.

"After shaking hands with about one hundred and fifty Christians, he turned to Omed and Ramke, and said, 'Brothers, where am I? Whom do I see and hear around me? When you two called on me at Gowahati, only a few years since, to inquire about this Christian religion, did I believe to live to see so great a fire of truth kindled in this dark land? No, never! But it is of God. On, my brothers, with the torch of truth, and you shall see all Garo-land ere long in a blaze.'

"By the close of 1870 there were two hundred and thirteen baptized believers among the Garos, organized into five churches. Since then, Mr. and Mrs. Keith, Mr. and Mrs. Phillips, Mr. and Mrs. Mason, and Miss Keeler, have joined the mission; Mr. Phillips has commenced a new station at Tura, one hundred miles farther into the hills than Gowalpara; and connected with the three stations there are nearly six hundred Garo church-members, all of whom would probably have been wild savages but for the orphan-asylum at Nowgong, and the unsuccessful tour of Mr. Bion, and the resolution of Kandura to 'hold on till death' at Gowahati.

"In 1871 Mr. Clark persuaded Godhula, one of his native assistants, to learn the Naga language, and explore the Naga hills. At first, neither man, woman, nor child, would speak to him. He was taken for a government spy, and his life was in danger. Gradually he convinced them as to his real object, and received a cordial welcome to hospitable homes, where a single room served as cook-room, sleeping-room, fowl-house, storehouse, and parlor, and to such delicacies as dried rotten fish, charred buffalo-hides, and putrid carcasses of cows and buffaloes. For several years he preached, and a number professed conversion. Mr. Clark made them occasional visits, and baptized. Then came a year of conflict between the Nagas and the British troops. Almost an entire exploring-party was massacred. (Among the Nagas, no one is thought very much of till he has killed some one.) For some time, no white man could be safe among the hills; and there were fears even for Godhula. Meanwhile there came rumors of defection among the disciples. At the first lifting of the cloud, Mr. Clark, accompanied only by a boy-servant, started for Haimong, a village on a hill twenty-seven hundred feet high, the home of most of the Naga disciples. No other native could be induced to go with him; for government could promise no protection. For ten months he remained among them without seeing a white face, sharing such accommodations as he could find, obliged to do his own cooking and mending; but at the close of 1876 he was permitted to rejoice in the founding of a new village *without heathen ceremonies*, where the Christian element was the ruling one, and to hear again the voices of inquirers and of converts testifying, 'Much sweeter than arrack and all pig-meat is the new doctrine.'

"From the Kohls and Chata Nagpore people — emigrants from Central India, of whom there are thousands in the Assam tea-gardens — nearly one hundred and fifty converts have been gathered.

"Among the Assamese themselves there has been little visible progress. There may have been *real* progress. Daily, from behind zenana curtains, eager eyes watch the coming of the lady-missionary; and men who at any time before in the past ten centuries would rather have opened a grave for their wives than a book now consent to their studying even the hated Christian books, if so they may learn to read.

"In 1873, Nidhi Levi, the first of Assamese converts, the best of Assamese poets, and one, at least, of the best Assamese preachers, passed away. A few months later Dr. Ward died, and still later Mrs. Bronson and Miss Bronson Cotes. The deaths of these early laborers bring more freshly than ever to our minds the marvel that what has been accomplished even in Assam has been within the active lifetime of a generation not yet past."

CHAPTER XIV.

THE TELUGUS.

"I BELIEVE I'd like to give up, and change places with Ida," said Katie.

Some weeks had passed since Ida left; but they had contained no missionary evening.

"'He that putteth his hand to the plough,'" Walter quoted: there was nothing in his face to tell whether in jest or in earnest.

"But there isn't any thing against those that *take their hands off* the plough, looking back," said Katie; "and I almost think I've done that."

Ida's last word to Kate, whispered with the good-by kiss at the depot, was, "Do *my* work, Katie, and more;" and the whistle cut short the explanation Ida meant, and Katie needed.

And Katie had tried. She had started a missionary sewing and reading circle among the girls before Ida left, and at first it succeeded famously: but now preparation for a church fair called for all spare moments; and, that day, a few of the leading girls had suggested that missionary reading was "not so interesting, after all," and, while they were engaged in fancy work, they had better read some of the magazines that would help them about it; and Katie, who knew the missionary reading *was* interesting, blamed herself for not making better selections.

Then there were the old people, and the sick, and the poor. She had finished four baby-aprons that Ida left unfinished; but two of them were laid away in paper boxes, for the mothers had no bureau-drawers, — laid away to be cried over sometimes, but never to be worn any more; and the other two were already torn and drabbled in the mud until they were of the same color with it and with those they had supplanted. The two most interesting old ladies had died too; and those who took their tenements could not speak a word of English, nor understand Katie's desperate attempts at German.

The whole work Ida had left her seemed like undertaking to train a flock of birds on the wing; for, in all the houses she visited, not a tenant was expecting to stay long. And the children grew more profane, and the men more red in the face, and silly in talk on Saturday nights, and the women more worn, and less interested in any thing but their own complaints and their neighbors' business. There were but two women in the lot that even seemed to wish for any thing better; and one of those had just moved away.

The sabbath-school class of semi-civilized vagabonds she had taken was full as when Ida left it, though half those in it had moved away; but the remaining half, on which she had depended for the civilization of new-comers, had, instead, been barbarized by them.

At last the one woman who seemed trying to do better, and whose every separate child wore some garment of Katie's making, came to her at night to borrow money, and, when Katie declined lending, turned away with mournful eyes, murmuring, "So I've received you kindly week after week, and taken your tracts, and that's all I get for it," and wended her way to the nearest groggery.

And that, or rather all this, was why she wished she could change places with Ida.

"One thing I am sure," she said: "the missionaries don't have to spend their lives in dragging their work by a long zigzag way forward, and then see things take a bee-line back where they were before."

"The work is one, you will find," said Mrs. Bancroft. "To-night, leaving Assam on the north, and starting at the head of the Bay of Bengal, we will sail south-west, past Calcutta and Serampore, past Orissa, till we reach the point where the coast runs almost due south. Landing here, we find ourselves among a people as manly, independent, and truthful, at least, as any of the new acquaintances we have made, and so energetic, persevering, and inquisitive, that they have gained the name of 'the Yankees of India.' Their country stretches seven hundred miles along the coast, and forms a semicircle, which at its widest point reaches three hundred and fifty miles inward; but detached companies of them may be found all over Southern India.

"In 1836 Mr. and Mrs. Day, the first missionaries sent them by the Missionary Union, arrived. Mr. Abbot sailed with them, destined for the same field, but was turned aside by the pressing claims of the Karens.

"In a healthful climate, with no opposition

from government, a beautiful language before them, sixteen million interesting heathen around them, and the glorious news of God's beginnings among the Karens reaching them by every mail, no wonder they commenced the mission hopefully.

"After Vizagapatam, Cicacole, and Madras had been tried, each for a short time, in 1840 we find them at Nellore. But change of time and place had had little effect on the Brahman gods. The congregations of from twenty-five to a hundred that gathered in the streets of Nellore met Mr. Day with the same objections, and dispersed to listen to the same lies, that assailed Carey in Bengal forty years before.

"'This is the Kali Yoga; we cannot be good in it;' 'Your religion is good for you, and ours for us;' 'We must live according to the rules of our caste; I am a Brahman, and cannot work; if I become a Christian, I shall starve;' 'When all the Brahman and great caste people believe, we will;' 'Show me your God, and I will believe;' 'If this religion is true, why have we never heard of it before?' — came from the people in answer to his most earnest appeals.

"'He will seize the lads sent to his school,

bind them, cram some of his food down their throats, and so break their caste;' 'He sprinkles a kind of powder in people's eyes, that makes them obey him;' 'He means to send the children to some foreign country,' — was the reward fame gave to his most generous efforts. Often, just as a congregation of eager, attentive listeners was gathered, some blustering Brahman would come in, raise an excitement, and transform them into a reviling mob. Once, while preaching at a festival, harder weapons than words were used; and Mr. Day was severely beaten, driven back through a narrow street, and barely escaped being trampled to death. Of course the assault was led by Brahmans.

"In March, 1840, Mr. and Mrs. Van Husen arrived. In July there came to Nellore a Telugu from a distant part of the country, for three years a believer: in September he was baptized. Two Tamils and an Eurasian had been baptized before. In October, 1844, a church of eight members, four of them missionaries, was organized at Nellore. Early the next year Mr. Van Husen, and a year later Mr. Day, left for America. Mr. Van Husen never returned.

"After ten years of hard work, the Telugu mission, in 1847, consisted of two disabled missionaries, with their wives in America, one Telugu convert, and three or four Tamils and Eurasians in India. Meanwhile Mr. Abbot, who was to have been Mr. Day's companion, from Sandoway was reaching out hands into regions where no missionary foot might tread, drawing in converts by the thousand, groaning over the harvest ripening without harvesters, and at last, broken down by the weight of the sheaves, had returned to America, and was pleading for money and men, not to sow barren soil, but to gather ripened fruit. We can hardly wonder to find the abandonment of the Telugu mission a subject of earnest discussion.

"The committee discussed, and threw the responsibility upon the Board; the Board discussed, and threw the responsibility upon the people. The people never kill a mission by a process more merciful than slow starvation: so in 1848 we find Mr. and Mrs. Day returning, accompanied by a new missionary, Mr. Jewett. During the voyage, their labors led to the conversion of the captain and one sailor; and, when they reached shore, many others were thoughtful.

"Two years passed, marked only by the slow failure of Mr. Day's health and the frequent illness of Mr. and Mrs. Jewett.

"But it could not be that the fifty thousand who had listened, at least once, to Christian preaching during the year, were quite the same as before. The missionaries *knew* it could not, and were hardly surprised, as the assistants James and Nersu returned from their village preaching, to hear in one place of several who were 'almost Christians,' and in another of a whole village which had abandoned idol-worship, and defended Christianity, though it did not practically accept it.

"The next year, Luchama, wife of the Telugu baptized by Mr. Day in 1840, after being for ten years a violent opposer, was converted, laid aside her ornaments, and united with the church. A little later we find her, with Julia, a boarding-scholar converted the year before, in a tent pitched by the wayside, aiding Mrs. Jewett in teaching Christ to the women who came to Nellore at the great festival. Soon after Julia was baptized, and one other, — three in four years.

"In 1853, when the failure of Mr. Day's health

again compelled him to leave, we find the abandonment of the mission again under discussion.

"The next year one of the assistants proved an apostate; and two years later, the other, Christian Nersu, died. Mr. Day never returned; but in 1854 Mr. and Mrs. Douglass sailed to reenforce the mission.

"By 1857 the church numbered twelve. Then came the great mutiny. Nellore was guarded only by three hundred invalid sepoys, whose captain said he could afford the missionaries no protection in case of attack. Mr. Douglass was already in Madras: Mr. Jewett went there for a few months. There was but one baptism that year.

"The next was a year of sunshine.

"First two women — Lydia, and Elizabeth, wife of Christian Nersu — applied for admission to the church.

"'This is all deception,' said a Mohammedan, witnessing their baptism.

"'I felt the power of the Holy Spirit coming down upon us,' said one of the sisters in the church.

"'I trembled exceedingly,' said another, not a Christian.

"Soon six others were baptized.

"'My heart overflows with joy,' said the woman who 'trembled exceedingly,' herself one of the number.

"'They will soon come in crowds,' said Polyappa, father of one of the six, a youth from the normal school; and soon he helped fulfil the prophecy by coming himself.

"Thirteen in all were baptized, nearly all of them from families connected with the school. It does not seem like a great work as we look back upon it; but it did to the missionaries then, and I think they judged rightly.

"In 1859 came a terrible visitation of cholera. Victims were found in the boarding-school and among the young converts.

"Often there was but a few hours' interval between perfect health and death. But it was hard to mourn for those who were so glad.

"'I am going to my Father,' said the woman who 'trembled exceedingly' when she stood for the first time by the waters of baptism, now fearlessly entering the river of death; and, turning to her husband, she asked the question no heathen can answer, 'Where are *you* going?'

"'O my Father, receive me now!' said another, the first pupil in the boarding-school, and a convert of the revival of 1858. 'I am ready. No fear, though a worm, and nothing. Come, take me now. Hast thou not said, He that seeks thee finds thee? Yes, Lord, I come.'

"'Why weep?' he said to those around him. 'I now enter heaven with great joy. Does not our Father want many to serve him above? I see the hosts of God. Don't you see them? O glorious city, how numerous are thy gates! Thanks be to God, who giveth us the victory!'

"Ruth, baptized from the boarding-school just before Mr. Day left, and now wife of Ezra, one of the most efficient native preachers, had been for eight years a consistent member of the church. In 1861 she became, for a little time, a member of Mr. Douglass's family.

"One morning, while the family were at the table, she began to tremble and weep as though her heart would break.

"'No one knows the cause of my grief,' she said as she arose and left.

"Through the afternoon she avoided answering questions; but about one at night she came to the room of Mr. and Mrs. Douglass, asking them to pray for her.

"'It was soon evident,' says Mr. Douglass, 'that we had more need of her prayers than she of ours. Such a scene we had never thought it would be our privilege to witness.' There was no more sleep. We had come to the gate of heaven.'

"'Truly,' said Mrs. Douglass, 'this is entertaining an angel unawares.'

"The next day, with a heavenly smile on her face, she went from room to room, from person to person, telling of the preciousness of Christ.

"For more than ten days this lasted, and the mission-house seemed the dwelling-place of God. The days were filled with work, and the nights with praise.

"'My child is mad; she is possessed of a devil,' said her poor old heathen mother in agony.

"But it was no madness. When the intense excitement was over, she settled down into one of the most earnest and happy of Christians. Her joyful experience was itself the fruit of weeks of earnest prayer, and within a few days bore fruit in the conversion of two. One of them, to the wonder of the world, was her own mother.

"The next year, two others were baptized; the next, four, one of them a brother of Ruth; then four more came, and then five. The dew fell very gently; but the years of absolute dearth were over.

"About seventy-five miles from Nellore lies Ongole, with a population of ten thousand. The missionaries had several times visited it, and awakened inquiries and an appetite for tracts and books among its people. One evening in 1854, after trying all day to gain a hearing in the city, and gaining only abuse and stones, Mr. and Mrs. Jewett and Nersu stopped on a hill overlooking the place, looked down upon its hundred temples, sang hymns of praise, and prayed God that he would send a missionary to Ongole, that souls might be saved there, and heathenism die.

"In 1860 it came at the same time into his heart and Mrs. Jewett's to go there again. They resolved to do it, trusting in God for means to meet the expense. Just then a friend came forward with two hundred dollars for 'extra expenses.' They went, and brought back with them to Nellore Obalu, a young man, the head of a family, a convert asking for baptism. He was baptized, and returned to Ongole.

"In 1862 Mr. Jewett, on his return to America, found the friends of missions again discussing the usual panacea for financial embarrassment,— the abandonment of the Telugu mission. The urgency of the case was stated to Mr. Jewett.

"'The Union may abandon the field,' he replied; 'but *I* will bear no part in the fearful responsibility. If encouragement and aid are refused me by the Union, then I will return *alone*, and spend my remaining strength and days among the Telugus.'

"'Well, brother, if you are *resolved* to return, we must send somebody with you to bury you; you certainly ought to have a Christian burial in that heathen land,' said the secretary with a smile.

"In April, 1865, the prayer of the little band that met on 'Prayer-meeting Hill,' never dreaming they were giving name to the place, began to be answered. Mr. Clough, the 'missionary for Ongole,' arrived with Dr. Jewett at Nellore. Mr. Douglass had been sick for months, and left immediately.

"Early the next year, Mr. Jewett and Mr. Clough visited Ongole. A while later, in Tala Kanda Pond, forty miles distant, just as he was sitting down to eat, a leather-dresser heard the news that a missionary had come to Ongole. The food remained untasted. Four years before, while away from home, he heard two of the native converts talking about religion. He hardly noticed what they said at the time; but as he walked home their words came to him again, and, as he afterwards said, 'the Lord enlightened his mind.'

"'I am resolved to give up idols,' he told his wife and neighbors.

"'Then Polarana and Maluchma will send cholera and small-pox among us; you are mad,' was their answer; and, for the months that followed, he was treated very much as if he had been a walking embodiment of both diseases.

"'If you cannot let me have the Christian religion here, I shall go away, and not return,' he said at last.

"'What is the Christian religion?' asked his wife.

"He told her what little he knew. It was very little, but enough to make her long to know more. And now they came together to Ongole as inquirers. Soon after, Mr. Jewett baptized them.

"The next year we see Mr. Clough on his pony,

and Mrs. Clough in her palanquin, the monotony of the journey varied only by the steady 'Ho, ho, hum' of the bearers, or an occasional extempore song from them on the supposed merits of Mrs. Clough and her little boy, placing seventy-five miles between themselves and all Christian society, except what they brought with them. No,

PALANQUIN-TRAVELLING.

not quite all; for at the door of the bungalow, running toward them, panting, laughing, capering like a little boy for joy, was Obalu. He soon left, and returned with hot water and sheep's milk: so, with coffee, and some mouldy bread brought from Nellore, they made their first breakfast at Ongole.

"'We thought it very good,' he writes. 'We

are very happy here; do not care to be any happier. True, we want money; but the Lord will send that.'

"Very soon two native preachers, in the midst of hard words, and sometimes hard stones, were offering the gospel to the citizens of Ongole. Every morning and evening there was preaching in some one of the villages around; while, three times a week, Mrs. Clough and Ruth went out together to talk on religious subjects with the villagers.

"On one of his first tours, about twenty years before, as Mr. Jewett with Nersu approached a village, a man came out and begged him to come with him. Following through mud and water, he reached a cluster of sixty mud houses, scarcely distinguishable from the earth around them, where a congregation soon gathered together.

"'Who made all these things?' he asked, after telling them of the fields of rice, the flocks, the men, the mountains, he had seen on his way. 'Did idols?'

"'No, God made them,' was the answer.

"'If your child,' said Nersu, 'should turn away from you to some other man, and say, "You are my father," would you not be displeased?'

"'Yes.'

"'That you have done to God.'

"'Tell us the parable of the vineyard,' said the guide, who had once visited the station at Nellore.

"He explained it, and that of the sower. Night came on, and he left.

"These were the pariahs, by the Brahmans falsely called 'outcast' or 'no caste' people. Among the Telugus they are divided into 'Malas,' who work as coolies, servants, woodcutters, &c., and 'Mardagas,' who are usually drummers, leather-dressers, cobblers, or something of the sort. Together they make one-tenth of the entire population. Their villages, numbering sometimes three or four thousand inhabitants, lay scattered all around. Often after that the gospel was preached in them. It was from one of them that the convert at Tala Konda Pond came.

"Presently from his region came the report that so often played the part of mirage on the missionary desert, — 'a large number of inquirers and remarkable interest.' But the man who was so overjoyed he could not eat at the thought of having a missionary within forty miles of him had made the best use of his rare privileges, and came often to Ongole; and he confirmed the report.

"On the 1st of January, 1867, a church of eight members was formed at Ongole.

"On the day the week of prayer closed, Mr. Clough and his assistant started for Tala Konda Pond. Three nights' travel by bullock-cart, with day-preaching in the intervening villages, brought them there. Stopping in a tamarind-grove, he sent word to the villagers that he had come to tell them of Jesus. The next day between thirty and forty men and women came, bringing each provision for four or five days, and an extra change of clothing.

"'We have come to learn more about Jesus,' they said; 'but we already believe in him, and want to be baptized.'

"Then came five days of preaching, Scripture-reading, prayer, and singing, never to be forgotten. The simple reading of the last two chapters of Matthew, or the remark, 'Christ died on the cross for our sins,' would affect the whole audience to tears.

"'I have seen many revivals at home,' said Mr. Clough, 'and witnessed many precious outpourings of the Holy Spirit: but I never saw such a blessed time as this; never saw such faith, and such love for Jesus the Saviour.'

"At the close, twenty-eight were baptized.

"The converts were from six villages, distant from twenty-five to fifty-five miles from Ongole. Returning to their homes, they met no pleasant welcome. A guard was placed at the entrance of their streets, forbidding them to pass either way. Water from the public wells was denied them; and, when disease appeared among the cattle, the Christians were accused of poisoning them, and taken before the magistrate. Mr. Clough stated the facts, the complaints were dismissed, and for a while the disciples had peace.

"Every thing was now put in the closest working-order. An earnest appeal for more missionaries was sent to America. Each village where there were convicts was directed to send one or two men to Ongole immediately after harvest, who should return and teach the rest. One native assistant was appointed to give his whole time to preaching in the villages; while Mr. Clough was busy by day, and often at night too, in receiving inquirers, and searching out hearers at Ongole, superintending the building of a chapel, and visiting the villages around.

"A little later, seven young men from six villages were gathered at the mission-house for instruction. Before the year closed, the Ongole church had grown from eight to seventy-five.

"Meanwhile, though to cholera were added famine and small-pox, the work went on at Nellore. Eleven were baptized in 1865, thirteen the next year; and the next, startled apparently by the thought that the founding of the station at Ongole and the death of the ablest assistant had thrown the whole burden on Mr. Jewett and the little church, almost every member organized himself into a private missionary society, and the result was thirty-three baptisms and three new out-stations.

"No human pen can describe the years that have followed,— years every day of which is a date in the record-book of heaven. The dying saint had given his rupee; poor blind Lydia, her four annas; the first Kala Konda Pond convert, his two chickens; the children, their egg-money; the poorest, something, till a spacious stone chapel was complete at Ongole. In the villages the demand for teachers and preachers was incessant. It seemed hardly right to make teachers of men who could only spell out words, and preachers of those who could do hardly more than say, 'Believe on the Lord Jesus Christ, and thou shalt be saved.' Many an educated American pastor would shrink back if duty called him to preach to an audience of sceptics, and courtesy allowed them to ask all the questions they thought during the sermon; yet to a work like this these ignorant but warm-hearted disciples were sent.

"No one felt the disadvantages of this course more keenly than the missionaries; but it was the best that could be done, and God blessed it. I wish we could follow these preachers, and watch the growth of gospel-fruit in each village. We can only glance here and there at the work, and then leave it.

"Here in Markapoor, eighty miles west of Ongole, the whole body of disciples had been seized, and sent to jail. They were whipped, fined three rupees each, and sent to work on the grounds around a Vishnu temple. One only escaped to tell the missionary.

"'Tell them,' he said, 'to bear it all patiently: when they go to work on the grounds, sing; when they go back to the prison, pray.'

"The message reached them; and prayer began.

"'That must be stopped,' said the Tasildar. 'Order them to work on the temple.'

"They were marched out, singing,—

> 'Pahpamoo dhulootsoo sume ;
> Puschathapamu kazoo sume.'

> 'Think of your sins, and pray for repentance;
> Fall at the feet of the invisible Jesus.'

"'That must be stopped,' said the officer; and they were returned to the jail.

"At once they began to pray.

"'Stop that!' came the order.

"'We cannot. The teacher told us to pray.'

"Again and again they were sent from jail to temple, and back; till at last the Tasildar, wearied either by their singing or the less musical voice of his own conscience, gave the order for their release.

"'But we cannot go,' they said. 'We have been fined and imprisoned unjustly. We cannot go out like criminals.'

"'How will you go?'

"'Let them give us the three rupees each we have been fined, and rice for seven days; then we will go.'

"The money was actually paid, the rice given, and the men went out triumphant, singing,—

'Pahpamoo dhulootsoo sume.'

"A dozen telegraph-wires could not have carried the news faster than it flew through that densely-settled country. Before six months had passed, Mr. Clough baptized one hundred and thirty within three-quarters of a mile of the jail; and now, within twenty miles of it, there are more than twelve hundred believers.

"Next we find Mr. Clough making a tour through these villages.

"At one time, just before midnight, he hears a noise like the running of a flock of buffaloes. He is just ready to lead his pony aside, and let the buffaloes pass, when, instead, he finds twenty or thirty men, all believers, gathering together to welcome him. Everywhere, whether in large towns, or hamlets whose name even he had not heard, he finds brethren or inquirers.

"And here at Garnegapeuta is a Christian village, with white houses, clean streets, and a neat schoolhouse built by the villagers.

"'In all heathen India, even among the Brahmans, you will find nothing to compare with it,' he says to the bystanders.

"Only one mud house remained neglected, and not whitewashed. It was the idol-house of the god Ramasawmy.

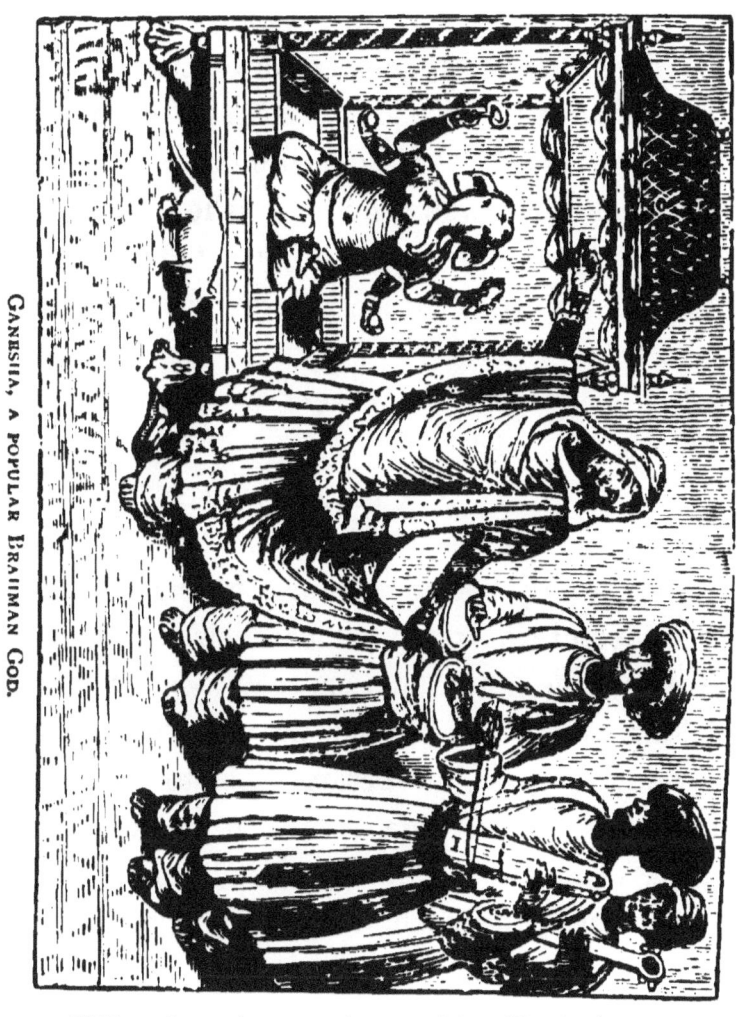

Ganesha, a popular Brahman God.

"'Why does it remain in this Christian hamlet?' asks the missionary.

"'If we pull it down, the heathen will be very angry.'

"'Let me do it, then.'

"In a minute a crowbar was put into his hands. After the first blow, helpers were plenty. In a few moments the house was a heap of rubbish. Two large slimy toads hopped out.

"'See Ramaswamy and his wife!' said one of the company in comic irony. 'Pretty gods, indeed! Let the heathen worship you: we don't want to.'

"And the toads were sent back among the rubbish.

"In the years that follow, we see him, now conducting alone a ministers' institute, with fifteen or twenty native preachers noting carefully every lecture as material for their sermons in time to come, for plagiarism is not yet a crime in Telugu preachers; now in some pariah village, carrying on the 'desperate, hand-to-hand contest with superstition, pride, prejudice, ignorance, drunkenness, lust, deceit, cunning, and every imaginable machination of the Devil;' now, alone at night, reasoning with some Nicodemus who 'believes, but dares not openly confess;' now galloping away from a crowd of heathen, the only way to stop entreaties for a teacher that he cannot grant; now making a long tour, baptizing three hundred and twenty-four before he returns.

"The first day of the week of prayer in Ongole was given to supplication for five hundred converts. The close of the year found five hundred and seventy-three baptisms.

"Converts multiplied around Nellore too; and the spirit of inquiry among the heathen, and earnestness among Christians, grew, until every Sunday afternoon, instead of holding meetings, the converts went out, visiting from house to house through the streets, or in the villages; and the covenant meetings were changed from records of Christian experience to reports of Christian work.

"The Timpanys arrived in 1868; in 1870, the M'Laurins and Mr. Bullard. The same year Mr. Timpany and his wife took up their abode in Ramapatam, a town of four thousand inhabitants, a little more than half way from Nellore to Ongole. Ezra and Ruth had gone there some months before to prepare the way.

"Fourteen years before, Mr. Jewett and Christian Nersu preached there, and were delighted with their attentive audiences.

"'Perhaps,' said Mr. Jewett, 'they may be of the Lord's elect.'

"'Yes,' answered Nersu. 'I was thinking in my mind, "Who are the elect?" Are not these who give such heed to the word of God?'

"Ten years later, after passing through it, Mr. Clough wrote, 'Above every thing else in India, except the blessing of God, I would like to see these two places' (Ramapatam and Allur) 'occupied by at least two of our missionaries.'

"Here Mr. Timpany started a school under a banian-tree, with sand for slates and blackboards, and forefingers for pencils. A little later, looking out upon the absolute darkness, he wrote, 'I sometimes cry like the prophet in answer to the question, "Son of man, can these dry bones live?" "O Lord God! thou knowest," my doubt going into my cry.'

"But before a year had passed he was able to report, 'We are in the midst of a constant revival.'

"At the close of 1871 there were two hundred and sixty-seven church-members connected with Rampatam. The next year, in a single tour in the neighborhood of Cumbaldiny, one hundred were baptized, and the membership grew to four hundred and twenty; and by the next it was impossible to go out in any direction without finding Christians in every two or three miles, while among the Mardagas scarcely an avowed heathen remained.

"In 1872 Mr. Clough left for America. A few evenings before his departure, five hundred representatives from the villages under his care gathered together for last words. Hours passed by, as hours will at such times, and half-past eleven came. The *very* last words must be spoken.

"Their courage failed. 'Don't leave us!' 'Stay with us!' 'Don't go to America!' burst from pleading lips, perhaps then, for the first time, realizing their loss.

"Others caught up the words; and from the crowd of eager petitioners, clasping his feet, pressing upon every side, came the same message, 'Don't go from us!'

"'See here,' said the missionary, turning to one: 'do you remember, when I was at your village, that you asked me to come again soon, and I told you that I could not; that I had one hundred and ninety villages to visit before I could see you again?'

"'Yes, yes!'

"'And do you remember that you begged me to send you a native preacher, and I told you I could not, for we had but eighteen, and they, too, must be scattered through all these hundred and ninety villages?'

"'Yes, yes!'

"'And, that finally, when you followed me out of the village, begging me to come, or send a preacher or teacher, I could do nothing but shut out your prayers, and gallop away?'

"'Yes.'

"'And was it so in your village?' turning to another.

"'Yes.'

"'And yours?'

"'Yes.'

"Memory had been only too faithful in recalling those scenes during the hours just past.

"'And now you know that I am worn out with work; that, unless I can rest, I shall soon not be able to visit you at all. You know, too, that we must have four new missionaries, and a theological seminary to train native preachers, who can stay with you all the time; and I must go to America to get the men and the money for the seminary.'

"The petition changed.

"'Go quick, and come quick; go quick, and come quick!'

"'When I am gone, will you pray every day that God will restore my health and Mrs. Clough's, and that he will send the four men, and the money for the seminary?'

"'We will.'

"So they parted, and the promise was well kept. Every day the Christians raised their petition, without a shadow of doubt that what they asked they should receive.

"And their prayer was answered. In less than two years, Mr. Clough returned with the last dollar of the needed fifty thousand pledged; and very soon four new missionaries — Mr. Williams, Mr. Downie, Mr. Campbell, and Mr. Drake — were at work in the Telugu field. Mr. Williams took charge of the seminary, aided by Rungiah, — 'one of the noblest of Christian men, an able preacher, pre-eminently godly, and with a model family;' and two others, 'young men of superior ability and sterling piety;' and in 1876 reported under their care eighty students, all strong, vigorous men, preparing to enter the field, and *work*.

"At Ongole Mr. and Mrs. Loughridge are laying the foundations of a Telugu college, and Mrs. Clough has charge of a normal school sustained by the Woman's Missionary Society, numbering fifty-nine scholars.

"During the past year a fearful famine has prevailed through Southern India. Everywhere, as they go forth to preach, the missionaries hear the cries of the starving; and much of their time has been given to obtaining relief. But neither famine, nor its attendant pestilence, has been able to stay the work. Within a year, seven hundred and twenty-four have been baptized; and the entire membership of the Telugu churches is now 4,394.

"'What a glorious wedding was that which was the stepping-stone to your coming to us in all the desolation of heathenism!' said Julia recently, on the occasion of the silver wedding of Dr. and Mrs. Jewett. 'You gave us the bloom of your youth, and now a light has been kindled which is spreading in all the country around.'"

"I wonder if there won't be an opening for a doctor there in a few years," said Walter.

"No doubt of it," said Katie. "I imagine they would want him to preach while he was practising, though."

"That of course," Walter replied. "He couldn't help it."

Mrs. Bancroft waited to hear more; but nothing more was said. Katie took a hand of each of the younger children, and led them up stairs, while happy tears dropped upon their clothing as she put them to bed. Grandpa Sears, with quick instinct, followed her out of the room, placing one hand on Walter's head as he passed. Clarence twisted a folded paper that he had held in his hand through the evening.

"Here's something I meant to have handed you before," he said, seeming not to hear Walter's words, — "a mathematical problem; your hobby, you know." As he passed Walter, he dropped the paper into his lap; then, opening the door, "It's a splendid evening for a walk, Charlie;" and Charlie, glad to take the remark as an invitation, accompanied him, leaving Walter alone with his mother.

"I sometimes think, that, at the best, we only help God, as Minnie helps you, by catching hold of the broom while you are sweeping," he said.

"But I am glad to know she wants to help; and, if there were no children to catch hold of brooms now, there would be no grown people to use them by and by. So she *does* help me, after all, unless I am very busy."

"And God is *never* very busy, — never too busy to train bunglers. There is comfort in that," said Walter.

And then he told how, one week before, he had settled the great question of life.

"And it is within that time that you have thought of being a missionary. Have you not decided hastily?" said Mrs. Bancroft after the first joyful half-hour had passed.

"No: it was long before then, — as long ago as when you told us about Judson and Price. I wanted to fill Price's place, only not to die so soon: I don't think martyrs are what is most needed now. That is what made me think of studying medicine."

"Do you mean that you became a Christian because you wanted to be a missionary?" asked Mrs. Bancroft. This inverted order of experience puzzled her.

"Yes: it seemed the only work worth doing, and the thought that I wasn't fit for it haunted me. I never wanted to do any thing before that I didn't think I could fit myself for, if I tried; but this I couldn't. And then I saw there wasn't any thing I was fitted for,— any thing I'd be satisfied to keep on doing forever, I mean. But I am satisfied now."

And so was Mrs. Bancroft. She rested her hand on his shoulder as, when he was smaller, she used to put it on his head, but said nothing.

"It's a long time ahead, and I can't tell what may happen. Maybe I shall find out it isn't my work, after all, as Katie thinks she has. In that case I'll stay at home and try to make money enough to hire a substitute at least. But I mean to keep where, if God *should* call me into the midst of the work, I could hear, and go without stopping to get ready. I think every one ought to do that."

Perhaps, with Mrs. Bancroft's thankfulness that Walter was ready, there was a little joy that so many years must pass first; a hope, that, instead of calling him to heathen lands, God would intrust to him the easier work of supplying the needed funds; for, after all, she was a mother.

CHAPTER XV.

TO-DAY.

KATIE was joyfully counting over her disappointments. She had hoped to fit herself for a missionary: instead, she had discovered her own unfitness, and found her true work. She had hoped that she might teach Walter not to watch her, taking her life as a test of the power of Christianity: instead, he had watched her more closely than ever; but he had become a Christian. She hoped, when grandpa Sears came, that his stay might be short: he was to spend his life with them; but her only trouble now was, that that life must be so short. She had hoped, that, since Ida had no good words for foreign missions, she might become content to say nothing about them: Ida was fitting for the work of a foreign missionary. She had hoped to see the conversion of her class: they were all scattered, and their places filled by new ones; but their letters told her they had joined other classes, and some had been led by other hands to Christ. She had hoped and prayed and planned for the success of her missionary sewing-circle: it had sunk in the preparation for the fair; but the sisters of the church, quickened by her evident disappointment, had organized a branch Woman's Missionary Society, and elected her secretary, and the contributions of the church were doubled.

"There isn't much use in our planning our work; the thing is to be willing to do it," said Katie.

"Is that so?"

In the darkness, Katie had imagined herself alone; but Walter had been on the sofa all the time, planning out *his* work.

"I have found it so," said Katie.

"Then I don't know but I may as well profit by your experience. I was planning how I could convince the world, particularly the small part of it called Clarence Merriam, that a man can be a missionary without being a fool."

"Is it very important that he should be convinced?" asked Katie.

The lamps were lighted, and in a moment Clarence came in. He was hardly seated with Walter and Katie before he commenced:—

"It is a melancholy fact, that though missions have been in existence for a century, and Christianity for nineteen centuries, not more than one-fourth of the world is Christian, and, of those, three-fourths are not Protestant."

Walter made no reply.

"You have given up your wild project of the other evening?"

"What would you advise me, then? What shall you do?" asked Walter. This was coming to the point much sooner than Clarence expected.

"I think I shall accept my uncle's offer, and engage in his cutlery,— book-keeper now, and agent by and by."

"It is a melancholy fact," remarked Walter gravely, "that though cutlery has been in use more than nineteen centuries, and forks for at least three, three-fourths of the world go without them, and, of the remainder, not one-fourth use silver ones."

"But the aim of missions is to do good, and of cutleries to make money: there is the difference."

"If your aim is *only* to make money, I would rather work at mine all my life and fail at last, than at yours and succeed."

"I did not mean that. Through money I can educate the ignorant, rescue the drunkard, succor the poor, reform the immoral, and relieve the suffering. I call those worthy objects, and there are organized channels for them."

"But people have been doing all those things for much more than a century," interposed Katie; "and at least three-fourths of the ignorant are still uneducated, the poor unsuccored, the immoral unreformed, and the suffering unrelieved. Every thing worth doing has to be done slowly. The things that can be done in one lifetime generally perish in another."

"I, too, believe in working for immortality," said Clarence; "but I think I can find a more practical way of doing it. I do not believe in spending four dollars to get one to the heathen."

"Do you mean that the managers of our missionary societies are dishonest or extravagant?"

"Neither: I only mean, that, for every four dollars given to missions, the heathen get not more than one dollar's worth of any thing worth having."

"Education is a commodity that has a market-value in America, I believe. In 1871 the pupils in mission schools of various denominations numbered 360,189.[1] In Massachusetts we spent that year for public-school education $12.10 per child.[2] At that rate, the education of those heathen children would cost $4,358,286: from which I infer, that at least so much of the $5,232,716 given to missions 'goes to the heathen;' at least four dollars out of five."

"A part of the expense of these schools is borne by the native Christians, is it not?"

"Yes; but if, as a result of missions, the money that would have gone for arrack and opium goes for schools; if natives are willing to pay for schooling, instead of being hired to send their children, as was done in the earlier days of missions,— the benefit conferred is at least as great as if we supported the schools entirely. Remember, too, that the stimulus to thought, which, according to Keshub Chunder Sen, missions have given, has sent hundreds to other

---

[1] Statistical tables in Land of the Veda, taken from reports of various societies for 1871.

[2] Report of Board of Education, 1872.

than mission schools, and that the idolatry supplanted *cost* something."[1]

"Yes," interposed Kate. "Mr. Douglass says, that in Bassein, for every dollar spent on dwelling-houses, markets, and buildings of real use, one hundred dollars are spent on pagodas, gods, and kyoungs. I fear it will be a long time before you will be able to complain of any such extravagance as that among the friends of missions."

"Still," said Clarence, entirely ignoring Katie's remark, "the object of missions is to save souls, not to educate children: and it is a fact, that every convert actually gained from heathenism thus far, even if we include the West-Indians as heathen, has cost $270; while in the harder countries, like Siam, they have cost $1,000 apiece."

"I gravely suspect that, if you count every thing, every orphan rescued by our asylums has cost more than $270; and I know, that, on an average, every drunkard reformed or lost one

---

[1] Some missions schools receive grants in aid from the British Government. On the other hand, should we count in the cost of private schools, endowed academies, normal schools, and new buildings, in Massachusetts, which is necessary to a fair comparison, it would fully double our estimate of the cost of education here.

really saved in our 'Homes,' every student educated in our colleges, every sick man cured at our hospitals, every rogue made honest by our reform schools, costs, on an average, more than that," said Katie. "But if you are consistent in your economy, and give up all these, I fancy we shall have a state of things you will not much like."

"It *would* be a melancholy fact," said Walter, "if the conversion of a soul cost as much as a really elegant silk dress or a horse; but, even then, I think there are members of our churches who could indulge in the luxury occasionally. Happily, however, the expenses of the Missionary Union, under which I shall enlist if I go, for five years in which I have estimated them, including every thing, from a theological seminary to a postage-stamp, were but $1,011,518; and the number baptized, 20,680, averaging $49 expense to each convert."[1]

"That includes some converts in European countries, does it not? India is the true test of the success of missions."

"The average expense in India, including

---

[1] Reports 1868-1872 inclusive.

Burmah, was $74 to each convert;[1] and this includes $10,000 for the Theological Seminary at Rangoon, and $13,000 for the printing-office and grounds there."

"Those must have been remarkable years."

"Not at all. There were no marked revivals, except that among the Telugus. I think the statement for the past five years would be even more favorable."

"Then you dispute my figures."

"No: I think them fair. For the first dozen years, either in the Bengal or Burman mission, the expenses were much more than $1,000 to each convert: I dare say that in both countries the average, including those years, and counting every thing spent on education as spent on missions, has been fully $270. There may be societies, especially where a very successful mission has graduated into independence, and a new and difficult one taken its place, whose average is greater than that now. Our Telugu and Chinese missions were founded nearly together.[2] For the twenty years prior to 1869, the expense of

[1] Charging those missions with the same proportion of the expense for officers, agents, &c., as they share in the special missionary appropriations of the society.

[2] Beginning with the Chinese of Siam.

the Telugu mission averaged more than $460 to a convert. Since then, the average cost has been $25. How soon we shall see a like sudden reduction in the Chinese mission, no man can tell; but, for the past, your estimate may be none too high."

"And you think it pays?"

"Certainly, if any thing does. The beginnings of all enterprises are costly. If you should count in all the money spent in machinery and fruitless experiments, you would find the first dozen sewing-machines, or any thing else worth having, cost more than $10,000 each. It does not follow that I shall not buy one at the present market-price, or that the thousands spent at the outset were not well spent."

"Still," said Clarence, "if more souls can be saved with the same money in other ways, I should, if a Christian, adopt those ways. The converts of home missions cost less than $50 each, while yours from heathenism cost $79."[1]

"Add to the expenditures of home-mission

[1] In estimating the future progress of missions by the past, converts who have died are, of course, deducted; but, in estimating the average expense to each convert, there is no propriety in this; certainly not if it is done for the sake of a comparison with home missions, and a like deduction is not made there.

societies those of our education societies, and to that the endowment of theological seminaries, the cost of half the literature (religious and secular) used in its field, of common, high, and boarding schools, in good part of orphan-asylums and other charitable institutions, then take away from their field the thousand indirect Christianizing influences, require them, like foreign missions, to create the conditions of success, and see on which side the balance would be."

"Then you would give up home missions?"

"Never! They are the true feeders of foreign missions. But it does not follow, that, because the parent supports the child, the child must be allowed to starve until the parent has eaten all that he possibly can. All I claim is, that, as compared with other benevolent enterprises, foreign missions are cheap; as compared with smoking, or fast horses, or following the fashions, they are extremely cheap; but, taking into account the eternity that lies before every soul, they are cheap beyond all possibility of comparison."

A brief pause, and Clarence remarked, "You have studied my problem evidently: have you solved it?"

"No."

"Have you it with you?"

Walter unfolded the paper Clarence had dropped in his lap on the last missionary evening.

"Read it, please."

Walter read, "In 1859 there were in the world 215,000 converts from heathenism, connected with forty-seven societies, whose period of labor has averaged thirty-nine years each. Dividing 215,000 by 39, we find the average annual gain of converts has been 5,538. The average annual expenditure has been about $1,500,000. The present annual expenditure is $5,000,000. At that rate, the annual increase would be 18,460. Supposing that the present rate of expenditure should continue, how long would it take to convert the 725,000,000 of the heathen world?"

Walter read without comment.

"According to my reckoning," said Clarence, "or rather that of 'The Index,'—for I am indebted to it for my figures,—it would take 39,273 years."

"Perhaps so. I have never learned to find the last term of a series in geometrical progression by addition."

"What do you mean?"

"I mean that your calculation is based upon a supposition absolutely unsupportable, — that contributions will remain the same, and converts increase at a fixed average rate; a thing which never has been, and never can be. Every true convert is a multiplier. Every converted community is a missionary force. During the first ten years after Carey landed in India, the average net gain of converts was two and a half per annum; during the last ten, 2,117. We should come nearer the truth if we say, that, on an average, the number of converts from heathen nations throughout the world has doubled every fifteen years; and, if it continues to do this, the year 2100 will open upon a converted world."

"Your arithmetic has run mad; you'd better muzzle it," said Clarence.

"It has been exposed to a bite from yours, I acknowledge. I do not think my estimate a basis for certain prophecy; though I do not believe you can find fifteen years in which the number of converts from heathenism has not doubled. I do not really expect the time will come when every individual in Heathendom, from an hour old upwards, will be a Protestant church-member; which is what your question demands. Remember, on the other hand, that an immense work of undermining has been done, not yet shown in numerical tables; that now there is a nominal Christian population in heathen lands nearly three times as great as the number of communicants; that, when the proportion of Protestant church-members to the population is as great as in America, — one in seven, — the work of foreign missions will be over; that, before that time, events may happen, — like the revolution in Madagascar, the voluntary opening of Japan, the evangelizing of the Catholic Church from within itself, the prevalence among the Hindoos of societies hostile to caste, the discovery of new tribes and eligible locations in Africa, — which will do in an hour the work that years have been waiting for; that, in fact, you might as well estimate the time it will take to go through Hoosac Mountain ten years hence by the time it took to *bore* through it at first as estimate the future progress of missions by the past or present progress. The sum of the whole matter is this." Walter read now from notes which he had been pencilling down during the conversation: —

"Missions do not go forward at a fixed, but at a constantly agumented, rate of increase. The reasons of this are, —

"1. The increasing number of converts, and therefore of contributions, in Christian lands.

"2. The increase of wealth in our country, shared in by the Church.

"3. The increase in general information and missionary zeal.

"4. The gradual undermining of confidence in idolatry among the heathen, which has been the main work of many societies in the past, but tells upon numerical tables only in the future.

"5. The removal of obstructions, such as the opposition of the East-India Company, the aversion to foreigners in China and Japan, the persecuting spirit of several heathen courts, the African slave-trade.

"6. Increased facilities for travelling in heathen lands, and communicating with their inhabitants through the press, enabling the missionary to do the work of many years in one.

"7. Increased knowledge of the geography, history, and religions of heathen nations.

"8. Improved methods of missionary labor.

"9. The fact that every true convert from heathenism is a contributor, to some extent, both in money and work.

"Many of these causes have but just begun to operate. Most of them are sure to operate more powerfully in the future than in the past. If they do, the child may be born in this century who shall live to see Christianity triumphant in India. But, if I believed the world would never be converted, I would still give to missions as I would to other works which I never expect to see finished, and believe it the most economical investment I could make."

"I am delighted to find such a serene hopefulness," said Clarence. "The only pity is, that it has no firmer foundation in reason." As this argument was unanswerable, both boys were glad of the entrance of Mrs. Bancroft; but, before she began her history, grandpa Sears interposed a word.

"Your figures are all right, Walter, and your conclusions may be. Perhaps God means to move his troops straight on to victory; but I doubt it. His cause always has rolled on, not shot forward like an arrow. And always some spokes in the wheel have been up, and some down; some going backward, and some going forward:

and those that were going up and forward have thought every thing was going in a bee-line to the goal; and those that were going backward have thought every thing was going backward, and the world to destruction. It has been first the conversion of the empire, then Popery; first the Reformation, then apostasy; first Cromwell, then Charles II.; first Edwards and. Whitefield and the great revival, then wide-spread defection and French infidelity. It needn't be so; but it it has been so. Missions have had no great set back yet; but I'm afraid. There are hours, when, if we put our hands firm to the wheel, years can do the work of centuries; and, if we don't, it rolls back, and the work of years or centuries must be slowly done over again. And I think this is such an hour. More men *must* be had in Burmah; and somewhere among our recent graduates there are ten men whom God calls to that field: but I'm afraid — because I am old and timid, maybe — that all our graduates haven't honestly asked, 'Is it I?' And there are the Telugus: either expenses must be increased to meet converts, or converts diminished to meet expenses among' them; and *we* must decide which. Somewhere in our land there are a thousand purses, that have yielded five dollars annually to our missions, that are called — just as really called of God as Samuel was — to decide it by opening wider, and yielding ten or fifteen; but I'm afraid there are members in our churches who are not seriously asking, 'Is mine one?' and, if they should find it was, wouldn't thank God for the discovery. And there are at least five thousand mothers whom God calls to train up their boys to think about missions, and be ready to go, if God calls them, as you are, Walter; but I am afraid some of them are not doing it. And the only way to insure that the whole amount of missionary energy shall double in the next fifteen years is for everybody to see to it that his own does."

"Had I closed the story two months ago," said Mrs. Bancroft, "it would have been in the same strain in which grandfather has just spoken; "but when, at the May anniversaries this year, I saw the people in the pews take up the debt of forty-seven thousand dollars which has been accumulating for the past eleven years, and of their own accord, with quiet obstinacy, hold the meeting in session against the will of its managers, till the greater part of the mountain was removed, and as I have since watched them patiently following up their work till the Missionary Union stands free, I have thanked God, *not* for the raising of the debt, but for the sure dawning of the day when the truth shall be universally received, that the work of missions is the business, not of a board or a society, but of every separate church-member.

"Let *us*, then, give a glance this evening at the work done and the work before us. We have seen that the India of to-day is not the India we visited with Carey in 1793. Then a letter twelve months old from England was new: now steam has brought London within thirty days of Calcutta, and the telegraph has reduced the distance to minutes. Then clumsy boats, the ox-cart, the palanquin, and the pony were the only aids to travel: now the railroads of India carry annually sixteen million passengers, her sacred Ganges is ploughed by government steamers, while twelve thousand miles of wire carry messages for her people. Then the whole interior was sealed, and its roads almost impassable: now it is all open, and surveyors are everywhere. Then no native thought of learning English: now it is hardly a barrier to an American professor, going among the educated classes there, that he speaks English only, while in the counting-houses of every large city may be found hundreds who read the language readily. Then a whisper against sacred customs through the mission press sent a panic through India and England: now changes more radical than the early missionaries dared dream are discussed weekly in *native* newspapers. Then children must be hired to attend Christian schools: now stanch Hindoos contribute to the support of these schools. Then, if natives could be induced to take Christian books as a gift, the missionary rejoiced in his success: books are sold now. Then the education of women was looked upon with terror or utter contempt: to-day the education of the girls of India receives more attention than did that of the boys thirty years ago, in Calcutta between seven and eight hundred women are regularly taught in their zenanas by the ladies of the Union Woman's Missionary Society, and many a young Brahman secretly imparts to his wife daily what he learns at the schools. Then no money could hire a respectable Hindoo to touch a dead body: now Brahmans in the medical schools practise dissection without a scruple. Then the Kulin Brahman honored his fathers-in-law by permitting them to support him: now he can be compelled to support his wives. It is not fifty years since the high-caste widow of India coveted the funeral-pile as the only door of escape from a fate infinitely more terrible: now, though at rare intervals, we hear of attempts at suttee; the intelligent classes look back upon it as we upon the human sacrifices of the Druids. It is not sixty years since an order was issued by the India Government, that missionaries 'must not preach to natives, nor allow native converts to do so:' now the officers of government and the founders of the Somaj vie with each other in praise of the work done by missions.

"And the change wrought, or working rather, is greater even than these outward signs indicate. It is no mere intellectual satisfaction that we feel when we find Euclid, Blackstone, Cowper, J. Stuart Mill, perhaps with the skin of the sacred cow used in their binding, resting on the tables of cultivated Brahmans, for by this we know that we have clasped hands with our Eastern cousins; that for the India of to-day every thing is possible. Already, in vision, we see, not afar off, the time when between us and them 'there shall be no more sea.' There could hardly be a more striking illustration of this change, which is the prophecy of greater change, than a little incident C. C. Coffin relates of a sacred Benares bull which strayed into the garden of a native Christian. The Christian split his head open. An angry Brahman dragged him before the court.

"'Whose was the bull?' asked the native judge.

"'Siva's.'

"'Then let Siva appear and make complaint.'

"'An earthquake cannot shake Benares; for it rests, not on earth, but on Siva's trident:' but the hand that holds the trident is growing unsteady; and, if it fails, what will become of Benares? Already within its gates are six hundred native Christians.

"'I question,' says Mrs. Bronson, returning to Assam through Calcutta after fourteen years' absence, 'whether in any country in the world so marvellous and so radical changes in the very foundations of the social and religious life of a people can be found as have occurred among the Hindoo population of British India during the last decade.'

"Do not imagine that the change thus working is already wrought. The old India has not passed away, though a new India is contesting the ground with it inch by inch. In city and in jungle, the present jostles against the past. The locomotive shrieks past villages built in the style of centuries ago, and in its course startles the tiger from his lair. Cow-catchers make irreverent but unmistakable suggestions to sacred bulls, and easy cushions and thirty miles an hour mar the romance as well as the hardships of pilgrimage; but the bulls are sacred still, and the pilgrimages are made. The gods are not rejected yet; though the time when men were ready to fight or die, or even to kill other people, for them, is past. Even now we need not go many miles from any of the large cities to find the wealthy Sudra dropping his offering into the brass plate of the Brahman beggar as humbly and reverently as though the dust of past centuries had never been stirred by the breath of the nineteenth."

"*Is* it the nineteenth century, the railroad, the telegraph, and the government schools, that have made the change? or do you claim the credit of it for missions?" asked Clarence.

"Both," said Mrs. Bancroft. "The question, so much discussed, has less interest to no one than to the missionary. Believing fully that the work of missions is the thing God meant when he made the world; that He who gave him his orders holds in his hand all the forces, moral, intellectual, and material, of the universe, — he claims the first right to the use of them all, and cares little where the credit is given, if but the work be done. For him the Suez Canal was dug; for him the railroad and the telegraph, the photographer's instruments, and the electrical battery, were designed by God long before they were discovered by man; for him all books are written; his is the cause for which the whole world is working to-day, except so far as its work is doomed to certain failure. But, in deciding the cause of the great change that has come over India, you must not forget that missionaries introduced there the first steam-engine, the first printing-press, the first native magazine and newspapers, the first girls' school, the first college, the first of a hundred other elements of civilization; and especially must you remember that to the hard work and persistent right living of the missionaries is due that conversion of the

English Government and the East-India Company without which these changes had been almost impossible.

"But, after all, our great joy is in the spiritual conquests of these eighty years.

"If the change in British Burmah and Southern India has been less marked than in Bengal, it is even more exclusively the result of Christian influences.

"The palace of Ava is a ruin; the prison of Oung-pen-la is overgrown with briers and cactuses; the hopia-tree at Amherst has fallen; the dwellings, the zayats, the graves even, of the earlier missionaries, are hard to find: but in fourteen hundred Burman faces lighted with the hope of immortality, in twenty thousand Karen and Garo hearts lifted to God in prayer, in hundreds of transformed hamlets from which more than four thousand Telugu converts send forth hymns of praise, they have a better memorial.

"And almost anywhere in British Burmah you need but to strike the shell of heathenism to prove that it is but a shell, though a very strong one still.

"'Our books tell nothing of the forgiveness of sins,' thoughtfully says a Bassein Burman.

"'Guatama is dead, and cannot help us; I want to know what Jesus Christ can do,' says another.

"'How remarkable it is,' says an aged Buddhist Pwo, near Rangoon, to a native preacher, 'that men and women of such intelligence as the teacher and mamma should leave their country and their comfortable houses, and come among us, who, in comparison, live like pigs!—how wonderful! We ought to run and beg them to tell us about God, instead of their living in a boat, and enduring hardships in going about to tell and entreat us. And yet, notwithstanding all this, we do not become Christians.' Here and there, as you enter a Burman house, you may find a copy of the Acts or Digest of Scripture, lying open, ready for reading when the master of the house comes in; and here and there in some Karen church you will find a steady, earnest Burman listener,—possibly one who has learned Karen that he might listen to Christian preaching.

"These are not Christians, perhaps will never be; for they fear the people: but, when the mass of the Buddhists are brought even where these stand, there will be no people to fear, and the greatest hindrance will be removed. This steady transfer from the ranks of opposers to the ranks of those who fear opposition is one of our brightest signs.

"And even now it is not sixty years since Judson was laboring, in peril of death, without one inquirer; not fifty since the Karens were without school or written language, a nation of drunkards; hardly seventy since Carey baptized his first convert. How long this gradual, I cannot call it slow, progress, this work of sapping and mining, shall last, I do not know, but not always. Some time, the battle shall be fought which shall be to India what Tours was to Europe, but not with material weapons. And the question for every Christian is, 'Shall I belong to the advance guard of Christ's army, or be a straggler in its rear?'

"It is lack of Christianity in America, not heathenism in Burmah, that now prevents the gospel from being preached in every town from Bengal Bay to China. We have not kept pace with God's providences. Our liberality has grown; but God's work has grown faster. While thousands of miles of territory are open to us now, that were hermetically sealed then; while, all over the mountains, tribes invite us that then would have received us on spear-points; while peoples then unnamed are building us chapels, and races that have sullenly withstood the labor of years are begging to join our ranks as laborers, — we have scarcely more than kept the ranks of our laborers filled as death has thinned them.

"Not less than I pity the heathen do I pity the men whom God is calling to help them, but who will not hear the call; for, notwithstanding our slackness, never was our part of Christ's great field so full of buds of promise as to-day."

A stray breeze sent the branches of the apple-tree against the window. It had been a white sheet of blossoms in the early spring: now the ground was strewn with embryo apples; but on the tree was little but leaves.

Grandpa looked at it, and then at Walter. "The drought, I suppose," he said.

"But God himself waters the trees of his spiritual orchard," answered Walter: "so there can be no drought there."

"God *gives the increase*," said grandpa; "and Paul has planted, I suppose; *but Apollos must water.*"

www.ingramcontent.com/pod-product-compliance
Lightning Source LLC
Chambersburg PA
CBHW020108010526
44115CB00008B/736